SCOTTISH GARDEN BUILDINGS

From Food to Folly

SCOTTISH GARDEN BUILDINGS

From Food to Folly

TIM BUXBAUM

MAINSTREAM
PUBLISHING

The publishers gratefully acknowledge financial assistance from the Scottish Arts Council in the publication of this volume.

First published in Great Britain 1989 by
MAINSTREAM PUBLISHING COMPANY (EDINBURGH) LTD
7 Albany Street
Edinburgh EH1 3UG

ISBN 1 85158 (cloth)

British Library Cataloguing in Publication Data

Buxbaum, Tim
   Scottish garden buildings: from food to folly.
   1. Scotland. Garden buildings
   I. Title
   728'.9

   ISBN 1-85158-113-8

Design and layout by James Hutcheson and Paul Keir.
Typeset in 12pt Garamond by Blackpool Typesetting Services Ltd., Blackpool.
Printed in Great Britain at The Bath Press, Avon

Contents

Chapter 1

The Growth of the Scottish Country Estate

A new landed class had been created in Scotland by the gift or sale of religious lands after the Reformation in 1560. That class was consolidated by King James VI, when he elevated his new professionals to become Lords of Erection in 1596, symbolising how the medieval aristocracy was being supplanted by men of talent or cunning, who fought less by arms and defensiveness, than by favour at court and legal writs. Thus the rise of the House of Argyll against the Macdonalds, and the rise of the Setons and the Maitlands. Many of the more innovative seventeenth century house developments were inspired by the descendants of these new men.

From about 1600, defensiveness in Scottish houses began to cede to graciousness, and graciousness to pleasure. Although there was no obviously fundamental change to the design of the tower house itself, parterres and knot gardens, sundials and fountains began to be spread around them, usually on their south side. If fortification was retained, it was more for imagery than for strength; thus the letter of 1632 from Sir Robert Kerr to the Earl of Lothian: 'by any means, do not take away the battlements, as some give me counsel to do, for that is the grace of the house, and makes it look like a castle and so noblest'.[1] The fashion for pantomime fortification ended after the Civil War, possibly in revulsion, and did not make a comeback for a further 100 years. No longer vertical or castellated, the elaborate new houses of the post-Restoration period expanded horizontally into the landscape. Existing piles were extended or reconstructed; by the standards of the Scottish economy of the time, substantial undertakings. The later seventeenth century saw the erection or the considerable extension of Hatton House, (near Edinburgh), Balcaskie (near Anstruther), Holyrood House, (Edinburgh), Leslie House, (by Glenrothes), Thirlestane Castle (Lauder), Drumlanrig Castle, Hamilton Palace, Kinross House[2], Caroline Park (Edinburgh), Dunkeld House, Moncrieff House (by Bridge of

Earn), Hopetoun House (South Queensferry), Melville House and Dalkeith Palace—to name only the greatest. The designs for these buildings came from a small group of architects, the first of whom was Sir William Bruce (*circa* 1630–1710), Surveyor General, and Overseer of the King's Works in Scotland between 1671 and 1678; followed by other celebrated architects—James Smith (*circa* 1645–1731), Alexander McGill (d 1734), and—eventually by William Adam (1689–1748).

Sir William Bruce was particularly well travelled[3]. He had visited France during the Commonwealth (during which it is alleged that he acted as a go-between between Charles II and General Monk), and he probably visited great French estates like Vaux le Vicomte, whose remarkable gardens, formed in 1660, comprised formal designs that included geometric *pièces d'eau*, fountains, topiaries, statues and knot gardens. What the Scots aristocracy had become accustomed to on the continent during exile was clearly influential upon their thinking when they came to review their estates on their return. The transformation was rapid. The drawings of Scottish houses and castles by Captain John Slezer[4], thought to date from 1672, showed that already many great Scottish buildings now formed part of a new, larger composition comprising terraces, parterres, walled gardens, and processional walks designed with an elaborate formality.

Cosmopolitan as such developments may have been, they were quite overshadowed by the operations of 'Bobbing John', sixth Earl of Mar, at his palace at Alloa in the early eighteenth century. The Great Garden, probably laid out between 1706 and 1714[5], was of a truly imperial scale, several miles in diameter from Alloa Tower in the west to Clackmannan Tower on King's Seat Hill to the east. The park lying between the Palace and the River Forth comprised an ordered layout of canals, parterres, ornamental trees and statues; becoming broader in context, with great avenues of trees and Wilderness further away. Daniel Defoe, when he visited it, regarded this garden as the finest in Scotland; but by then the client was abroad, having led the unsuccessful Jacobite rebellion in 1715 to an indeterminate conclusion at Sherrifmuir. Mar spent the remainder of his life in exile. In 1729, John Macky paid a visit.

The plantation . . . is the largest and finest . . . of any in Britain. It far exceeds Hampton Court or Kensington, the gardens consisting of two and forty acres; and the wood, with vistas cut through it of 150 acres. The entry from the Town is from the West by a pair of fine stone gates, through a spacious avenue, which leads you to an area fronting the house on that side, in the middle of which is a gladiator, after the manner of that at Hampton Court, and on right hand of this Area is a spacious Garden with fine terras and Bowling Green, adorned with the largest evergreens you can see anywhere. To the south of the house is the parterre, spacious and finely adorned with statues and vases, and from the parterre to the River Forth runs a fine Terras or Avenue; from whence and from the parterre, you have 32 different vistas, each ending on some remarkable seat or mountain at some miles distant; one of them shows you Stirling Castle at four miles distance, another the palace of Elphinston [Dunmore Tower] on the other side of the river; a third the Castle of Clacmanig [Clackmannan Tower]; and so the rest; in the middle of this long terras is a basin of water, like that of the Duke of Chandois at Channons, in the middle of which is the Statue of Cain flying at Abel; and at the end to the river are a pair of pyramidal gates where a ship of 300 tonnes may unload. The avenue to the east through the wood is prodigiously long and large, and between each vista, from the parterre, are wildernesses of trees for birds, and little grottoes; the house was not yet quite finished; but by the great staircases from every front, one can guess at its grandeur.[6]

Rural Economy

The country estate was the centre of the local economy, its income and grandeur depending very much upon efficiency of cultivation, and the state of the soil. Almost certainly, money to pay for the growing elaboration of the estates derived from increasing agricultural efficiency, consequent upon enclosure and investment. Prior to that, tenants worked the rigs, typically strips of land up to two miles long, manured or treated with seaweed, and rarely allowed to lie fallow. Multiple tenancies had been frequent, and the community relied upon communal oxen, communal bean fields, marlpits, quarries, osier beds and small vegetable gardens. There seems to have been no field cultivation as we now know it.

There was a severe shortage of trees, and the lack of shelter probably affected the productivity of the soil which, in many cases, seems to have been suffering from exhaustion due to extensive rig cultivation. Up to the early eighteenth century, little timber seems to have been planted. On the contrary, woods in the Borders had been cleared by King James VI to destroy the cover of brigands or "moss-troopers"; and the park of oak trees at Falkland Palace had been felled by Cromwell's troops during the Civil War for use in the construction of a barracks and citadel at Perth. In 1729, John Macky mocked the park at Holyrood:

> The park belonging to this Palace is about 4 miles in cir-
> cumference; but what is very comical, there is neither beer
> (barley) nor tree in it; it is wall'd round with a stone wall, and
> yet there is nothing in it but high mountains cover'd with
> grass.[7]

In the words of William Mackintosh of Borlum, the country was virtually 'destitute of woods, some shires entirely without a bush or a stick in it . . . the nation being entirely destitute of forest, or indeed any Quantity of Woods to furnish Burnwood'.[8] Although legislation which required freeholders to oblige their tenants to 'plant woods, trees and hedges, and sow broom in convenient places' was reinforced in 1716, and although those who damaged trees risked a public whipping from the common hangman, success in the early eighteenth century was sporadic. Dr Johnson, accompanying James Boswell around Scotland in 1772, discerned no tree between Montrose and Aberdeen, and was 'repelled by this wide extent of hopeless sterility . . . the Oak and the thorn is equally a stranger, and the whole country is extended equally in nakedness. A tree might be a show in Scotland, as a horse in Venice'.[9] One explanation was offered to Boswell by Lord Hailes: 'Before the Restoration, few trees were planted, unless by the monastic drones; the successors (and worthy patriots they were), the barons, first cut down the trees, and then sold the estates. The gentleman at St Andrews, who said that there were but two trees in Fife, ought to have added, that the elms of Balmerino were sold within these 20 years to make pumps for the fire engines'.[10]

It is not surprising that a key part of eighteenth century agricultural improvement comprised the large scale planting of trees, and the deliberate establishment of park land in the neighbourhood of the big house. Fifty years before Johnson, Defoe had spotted change in the Lothians: 'You hardly see a gentleman's house, as you pass the Lothians towards Edinburgh, but they are distinguished by groves and walks of fir-trees about them; which, though in most places they are but young, yet show us, that in a few years, Scotland will not need to send to Norway for timber and deal, but will have sufficient of our own, and perhaps be able to furnish England too with considerable quantities'.[11]

Initial dependence upon native sycamore, birch, Scots pine, oak and ash was broadened with new species such as horse chestnut, introduced first at Stobo and at Dawyck in 1650. Sir John Clerk (1676–1755) who planted 300,000 trees on his estate at Penicuik, just south of Edinburgh, between 1700 and 1730, described his intentions thus: 'If the planting grow, and the Avenue terminat on any object, such as a porch or ruine, it will make, in time, a very good figure from the House, for 'tis to be observed that since the House of Pennicuik is situated on a high, cold, wild ground, it can be in no way so much improven as by planting'.[12] Tree planting became competitive. James Farquharson of Invercauld is said to have planted two million larches and sixteen million firs at Braemar between 1760 and 1806; between 1767 and 1781, the ninth Earl of Moray planted eight million pines at Darnaway, near Forres; while John, fourth Duke of Atholl, earned his nickname 'the planting Duke' by covering sixteen thousand acres at Blair with over twenty million trees; steeper hillside was planted by firing seeds from a cannon below.

The layout of such plantations (presumably those far from the cannon) was viewed in terms of a strict geometry. The 1720 design for Taymouth was based on six avenues of trees radiating from the house a mile in each direction. William Adam's design for his own estate of Blair Adam, near Kinross, took the form of squares, circles and triangles of trees, up to one hundred acres apiece, planted apparently without any regard for the lie of the land.

Man's confidence in his capacity to improve nature extended from the formal plantation of trees to the reconstruction of nature herself. The second Earl of Stair, having acquired a taste for gardens in the French style while ambassador at Versailles between 1715 and 1720, employed troops to fulfil major landscaping schemes at his estates of Newliston, near Edinburgh, and Castle Kennedy near Wigtown. The soldiers created ponds, cascades and canals, and constructed large-scale earthworks with such exotic names as the 'Giant's Grave', 'Mount Marlborough', and the 'Dancing Green'. The fashion caught on. In 1729, John Macky witnessed estate workers at Dupplin 'filling up a deep precipice between two hills, to make them regular'.[13]

Agricultural Improvements and Enclosures

From the late seventeenth century, accessible Scotland gradually changed in character from rigs and bogs to enclosed fields; a process often triggered as estates were consolidated through inheritance, marriage and purchase. The first estate enclosure may have been at Lennoxlove, near Haddington, from 1674. Yester, which followed two years later, enclosed some million trees by walls eight miles in circumference; so impressive as to earn the following compliment from John Macky in 1729: 'The best planted park I ever saw, larger and as well walled and more regularly planted than Richmond'.[14]

Enclosure was encouraged by the Scots Parliament in the 1695 'Act Anent Lands Lying Runrig', but the removal of tenants from their traditional homes caused social unrest. The activity, and the popular reaction to it, are well summarised in the title of a 1720 Act[15]: 'To encourage the planting of timber trees, fruit trees and other trees, for ornament, shelter or profit; and for the better preservation of same, and for the Preventing of Burning of Woods'. Those who cut, burned, breeched, destroyed, or spoiled plantations, hedges, trees or ditches would be liable for severe penalties. The discontent culminated in the Levellers Rising of 1724, and an outburst of anger at the annual Horse Fair at Kelton Hill in Dumfries, which culminated in the pulling down of new dykes. Tenants

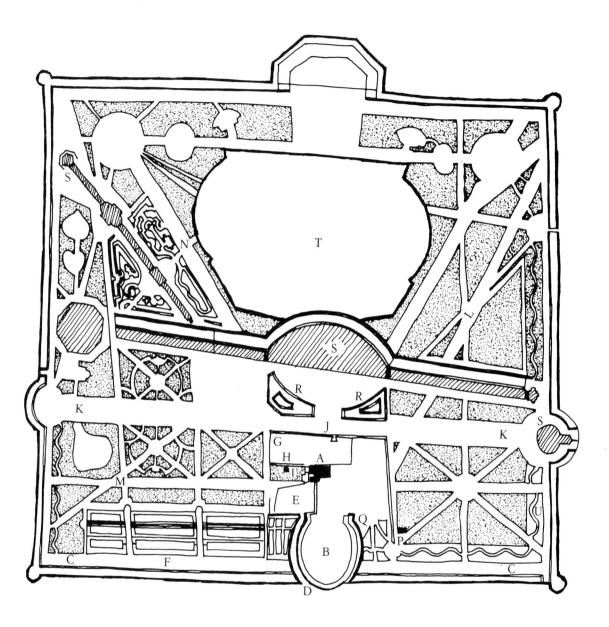

Newliston House. Drawing based on the 1759 copy (now in Blenheim Palace muniment room) of the original garden plan circa 1725 by William Adam. Note the importance attached to views out of the garden.

For notation, see end of Selective Gazetteer.

13

uprooted new young trees which they felt impoverished the soil, stole the sunshine, and harboured destructive birds. The most troublesome Levellers were transported to America.

There was some debate among the Improvers as to the most effective methods of enclosure. Mackintosh of Borlum rejected enclosure by stone walls, as was the practice in the Lothians, judging them bleak and liable to decay as soon as they were completed, necessitating immense labour to build, and providing no winter feed. He preferred enclosure by hedges of whitehorn quicksets, (so rare that they had to be imported from nurseries in England and Holland), as a bonus, fruit trees could be planted within the hedges. Thorn hedges were subsequently planted in their tens of thousands.

Short leases and high rents had produced a tenant mentality that led Borlum to conclude that it 'does not care how ill he uses every part of his farm, that it may look as despicable as possible; instead of improving it, it is worse this year he goes out, than it was when he came in. What must a country come to, that annually sinks in value?'[16] It was a vicious circle. Enlightened landlords were given a lead by Adam Cockburn of Ormiston (1656–1735), Lord Justice Clerk. In 1698, he granted an eleven year lease to Robert Wight, and tradition holds that Wight was the first tenant farmer in Scotland to enclose land with a ditch and a hedge, and to plant trees in the hedgerows at his own expense, for his own benefit. The estate at Ormiston seemed to prosper, to such an extent that by 1733 it could be observed that 'All is now enclosed, and most of the fences efficient; and the farmers have become wealthy far beyond the common condition of persons of their rank'.[17] John Cockburn, Adam's son, introduced a system of letting to tenants for the period of 'three lives', which would permit three generations of tenant farmers to invest in successive improvement. In 1736, Cockburn went on to plan a model village at Ormiston designed to encourage cottage craft industries, the production of quality textiles, brewing and distilling. But visionary schemes like this were expensive, and Cockburn was somewhat naive. Like a number of early improvers, he suffered considerable financial difficulty and, faced with bankruptcy, sold his estate to the Earl of Hopetoun.

Scotland was generally backward in agricultural practice. John

Walker of Beanston, regarded as the 'father' of fallowing in Scotland, began to allow his fields to lie fallow, in rotation, in 1690; but it took a long time to gain widespread acceptance. Thirty-five years later, Defoe could still record with sorrow that the Scots failed to fallow their land or fold their sheep. Lairds did not find it easy to persuade tenants to undertake the enormously laborious undertakings of liming, draining, and fertilising marsh, sandy heathland or strong clay.[18] Consequently, a number of improving lairds began to import farmers and labour from England. The Duchess of Gordon is credited with being the first, importing English ploughmen and ploughs to work on her estate in 1706. Sir Archibald Grant of Monymusk brought Thomas Winter north from Norfolk in 1726, to act as land surveyor and landscape gardener. Yet three years later, Mackintosh of Borlum felt it necessary to state in his *Essay on Ways and Means of Inclosing, Fallowing, Planting etc in Scotland*: 'it is our Case, Poverty, Inconveniences and Ugliness have, for several Years overrun ours, and need we blush to ask Assistance from Neighbours?'[19]

Once advice from England had been absorbed, answers to agricultural problems began to be solved from within Scotland itself. The Society of Improvers of the Knowledge of Agriculture in Scotland, the earliest such body in Europe, was founded in Edinburgh in 1723; and its members included senior figures in Scots life such as the Dukes of Atholl, Hamilton and Perth; and the Earls of Haddington, Stair, Findlater and Wemyss. Many other agricultural societies followed. The new mood for improvement was exemplified by the Earl of Islay, who purchased an estate consisting mostly of bog, at Whim, near Peebles, in 1729. He immediately set about to improve it by draining, planting, and forming ornamental lakes, as Robert Maxwell of Arkland recorded, 'The Earl of Islay has shown an example of agriculture that was much wanted. His Lordship made choice of Moss, almost everywhere in the Kingdom neglected, knowing that, being made up of excellent Materials, it is improvable, on a moderate Expense, from a very small to a very great value'.[20] A portion of the original bog was left within the walled garden at Whim, as a trophy to be appreciated by future generations.

In 1725 the tenants at Blair were obliged by their tacks (i.e. leases) to 'sow pittatoes, turneps, and carots, to thatch their biggings with heather, to enclose an acre or two of their ground yearly, to plant twelve young trees yearly, and to build ston or clay chemneys in their houses and to sow pease'[21]. With the planting of shelter belts, the drainage of mossy bogs, the fertilising of difficult ground, and the construction of boundary walls with stones cleared from the fields, the formation of a new geometry in the Scots landscape began in earnest.[22]

The Early Landscape Movement

Once the grounds beyond the walled garden were tamed and cultivated, there followed a reaction against the artificiality of the formal terraced gardens of the seventeenth and early eighteenth centuries. It had proved to be an expensive form of gardening, absorbing labour that could otherwise be used for agricultural improvement; and its potential had been exhausted. Out went the parterre, the terrace, the gazebo, the knot garden, the garden pavilion and the associated buildings. Landscape became more flowing, and there arose the idea that nothing should be obvious; the landscape should unfold, and anticipation be heightened by distant glimpses of mysterious structures, chimneys and roofscapes. The new ideal was expressed by Alexander Pope:

> He gains all points who pleasingly confounds,
> Surprises, varies, and conceals the bounds.

Man now sought to exploit the wonders of nature as an equal partner, and to enhance it by imagery and associations from the past. The intellectual base of the new movement was provided by Stephen Switzer, Charles Bridgman (inventor of the ha-ha with William Kent), and Batty Langley. They spurned as 'shocking' the boring predictability of the 'stiff, regular' formal gardens: 'After we have seen one quarter thereof, the very same is repeated in all the remaining parts, so we are tired, instead of being further entertained with something new'.[23] Instead the new designs should provide 'new and delightful scenes with every step taken'. Langley, yearning for gnarled oak trees in preference to a garden of 'trifling knots',[24] desired a communion with a carefully manicured nature. So did Sir John Clerk of Penicuik: 'the meadows are filled with every kind of field herbs, and watered with perennial streams. Therefore a multitude of tame animals, especially horses and oxen, are seen, not so much to graze as to disport themselves. The woods are in leaf with every kind of tree. Wild animals, whether quadrupeds or birds, not only endure the sight of man, but, as it were, court his society'.[25]

The new fashion sometimes required the re-ordering of only recently created landscapes. The late formal gardens at Yester, near Gifford, designed in 1751, were changed only two years later. In 1754, Thomas Winter was instructed to modify and soften the original layout created at Taymouth by William Adam twenty-two years earlier. Sweeping new parkland necessarily entailed the removal of formal gardens, ornamental cascades and canals, and that is what happened both at Yester and Arniston.

There was a clear growth of expertise among landscape gardeners, and in the respect for their expertise by their patrons. Robert Robinson worked at Crathes Castle, James Robertson at Dalhousie, Alexander Nasmyth at Blair and Dunglass, and the prolific Thomas White and his son at Scone, Keir, Allanton and Duns. Formal gardens adjacent to the house were translated into walled gardens at some distance; and formal water features and canals were softened into natural lakes. The house now stood alone, like a classical villa in an Italianate landscape in a formal relationship to water, hills, and other seemingly natural (but usually man-made) features. The view from the house was intended to create the image of pictorial space, offering framed views and enticing glimpses.

After 1762, the mood changed and Scotland gained a new imagery. Before then, eighteenth century travellers to Italy might have admired the spectacular scenery of Alpine passes, but had failed to perceive any attraction in leaving the rational landscapes of England for the wild, rude (and thereby backward) Highlands of Scotland. They would find the Alps sublime, but would regard the Highlands as a wasteland of boggy forests, swollen rivers, Gaelic-speaking inhabitants, with a primaeval culture and a hostile land-

An eighteenth century vision of sublime Highland scenery.

scape. Experienced travellers like Thomas Pennant came equipped with trinkets and guns to deal with the natives.

The publication of the Ossian epic poems by James MacPherson in 1762 changed all that. The Highlands were suddenly revealed in their glory, as the home of noble savages, sublime in their landscape and their Dark Age oratory. Although MacPherson may well have embroidered drastically upon genuine original oral traditions, the spirit of romance and awful scenery which he conjured up was received with rapture. The undisputed fact of the survival of oral tradition in this remote spot kindled the imagination of people throughout Europe. Travellers flocked to experience rushing water-falls, precipitous hillsides and mossy caves. As communication improved, they were able to enjoy the "horrid" aspects of nature from relative comfort; and anything that could be done to enhance that horror was welcomed. Sensations of awe and mystery awakened by the artificial grottos within private gardens (such as the 1708 grotto at Yester and the 1726 grotto at Arniston) could now be enjoyed in the raw. Travellers to Scotland relished wild landscape and natural wonders, of caves, of chasms, gorges, cliffs, and—perhaps the most famous of all—the whirlpool at Corryvreckan. They arrived with a sense of heightened expectation, which—on occasion—remained unfulfilled. With a certain sense of mockery, Pennant thus describes his visit to Hoddom Castle: 'instead of finding a captive damsel and a fierce warder, met with a courteous Laird and his beauteous wife; and the dungeon not filled with piteous captives, but well stored with generous wines; not con-demned to a long imprisonment'.[26] In 1787, Robert Burns joined the growing number of visitors to the dramatic Falls of Bruar, at Blair, and dedicated a poem to the Duke of Atholl, in 1787, recom-mending that a plantation of trees would enhance the scene:

> The Humble Petition of Bruar Water
> to the Noble Duke of Athole
>
> My Lord, I know your noble ear
> Woe ne'er assails in vain;
> Embolden'd thus, I beg you'll hear

> Your humble slave complain,
> How saucy Phoebus' scorching beams,
> In flaming summer-pride,
> Dry-withering, waste my foamy streams
> And drink my crystal tide

In expectation that the requested planting will be carried out, the poem concludes;

> Here, foaming down the shelvy rocks,
> In twisting strength I rin;
> There high my boiling torrent smokes,
> Wild roaring o'er a linn:
> Enjoying large each spring and well,
> As Nature gave them me,
> I am, altho' I say't mysel,
> Worth gaun a mile to see.
>
> Would then my noble master please,
> To grant my highest wishes,
> He'll shade my banks wi' tow'ring trees,
> And bonnie spreading bushes.
> Delighted doubly then, My Lord
> You'll wander on my banks,
> And listen mony a grateful bird
> Return your tuneful thanks.

In 1796 the Falls were duly planted with larch, spruce and fir, and dressed with a complementary array of summer houses and viewing pavilions.

In the late eighteenth century, landscape theorists split into two camps: adherents of what Uvedale Price had identified as the 'beautiful', consisting of smoothness, undulations and so on; against those who preferred the 'picturesque', with its roughness, disruptiveness and sudden variation. The debate, increasingly acrimonious in England, was codified by Richard Payne Knight as between the 'garden undressed' (picturesque and wild with only minimal intervention by man); and the 'garden dressed in the modern style' (in which man used his skill to adapt nature to his own ends). The former held the house visually secondary to nature; whereas the latter rendered nature secondary to an overall plan.

Estate Improvement

Picturesque landscapes still had to accommodate a large number of new utilitarian structures, occasionally of the highest architectural distinction. They included courts of offices, stables, steadings, walled gardens and—later—home farms. The landscape was enhanced by strategically placed pavilions and buildings of a variety of symbolic or leisure uses: temples, viewing platforms, bath houses, obelisks and mausolea. The technical achievements of improvement attracted every bit as much attention as did the aesthetic additions to the skyline.

By the end of the eighteenth century, Scottish farms, from having started with a handicap, were now held out as a model for English ones to follow. With the true impartiality of a London-based Scot, John Loudon (1783-1843) enquired: 'What is meant by the Scotch system of laying out farms adapted to England? To this I answer that agriculture in Scotland is conducted upon more scientific principles than in England: that it has attained to a higher degree of perfection, and that, consequently, buildings and other adjuncts necessary to its operations, are better calculated for effecting the proposed end'.[27] Loudon was clearly referring to the influence of the various Farmers Clubs and Agricultural Associations. A tremendous improvement had taken place within living memory in what had been thought to have been uncultivatable territories—particularly in the Great Moss of Forth. To celebrate his achievement, one such improver—the enlightened owner of Blair Drummond, Henry Home, Lord Kames, erected an obelisk with the following inscription: 'By Henry Home for his neighbours as well as himself who this obelisk erected. Graft benevolence on self-love—the fruit will be delicious'.

As the nineteenth century progressed, country-house economy became transformed by new technology and by the effects of improved road and rail communication. Previously untillable soil could now be fertilised, bogs drained, and crops exported. Landowners could order, and have delivered, iron ploughs, clay drainage pipes, entrance gates, and any implement they wished or could afford. It released them from the previous dependence on the estate blacksmith or carpenter. Aesthetic senses could be indulged by ordering quantities of urns, balusters, and other architectural ornament from the artificial stone manufacturers.[28] A vast array of casting was turned out by the furnaces; the 1889 Boulton and Paul catalogue offers a choice of cast-iron chrysanthemum houses, stables, piggeries, boathouses, cartsheds, even a combination shelter for pet birds, rabbits and guinea pigs. Those with grander ambitions, could buy bear and kangaroo houses, cast-iron fountains, fishing temples, tennis pavilions, and gates with spear railings. A two-bedroom-and-larder cottage for a gardener, gamekeeper or labourer could be had for approximately £150. The firm's patrons included the Marquess of Bute, the Sultan of Turkey and the Marchioness of Lothian.

Cultivation was equally revolutionised by the speedy development of steam power from about 1800, which transformed the capability of estate industries such as the sawmill, the quarries and the mines. Improvements to steam heating now made viable the creation of extensive networks of heated glasshouses for fruit, vegetable and—particularly—ornamental bedding plants. By the mid-nineteenth century, some estates had begun to generate their own gas for domestic lighting, and by the end of the century, it was not unusual to find an electricity generating house among estate buildings.

The Victorians reacted against the landscape movement and reintroduced a version of the earlier formal gardens, adapted for the brilliant new bedding plants. Charles McIntosh, head gardener at Drumlanrig, set out the new philosophy:

> A pleasure ground in the modern time differs from that prevalent at any former period in including all the scenes and sources of enjoyment and recreation of the ancient style, as well as the modern. For example, adjoining the Drawing Room front, there is a terrace . . . with or without an architectural flower garden, decorated with statues, vases and fountains.

> Beyond this . . . may be a lawn with flowers, shrubs, groups of trees, ponds, lakes, rock work, summerhouse, or greenhouses, an orangery, and sometimes a botanic garden. Walks may stretch away . . . to a shrubbery which . . . is usually formed into an arboretum, containing all the hardy trees and shrubs which the extent of the scene will admit; and in the course of the walk through the scene, there may be rustic structures, such as woodhouses, moss houses, root houses, rock houses, or cyclopean cottages, Swiss cottages, common covered seats, exposed seats of wood or stone, temples, ruins, grottoes, caverns, imitations of ancient buildings; and, in short, there is scarcely an architectural object capable of being rendered ornamental and a shelter from the sun, the wind or the rain, which may not find a place.[29]

When the Victorians determined upon a course of action, they prosecuted it with vigour. The gardens at Keir, by Bridge of Allan, are every bit as spectacular in their own way, as had been the Earl of Mar's Great Garden at Alloa. Smaller and more compact, the Keir policies offer an intricate pattern of gates, terraces, viewing platforms, pergolas, tunnels, bridges, a water garden, a water house, a bath house, walled gardens, gazebos, sundials, rustic gates, rustic bridges, steps, urns, statues and a yew house. This remarkable world of fantasy is occasionally open to the public under Scotland's Gardens Scheme.

In the later nineteenth century, the growing middle class who could not quite aspire to their own country houses, congregated in fashionable new towns like Helensburgh, and suburbs like Bearsden, in architect-designed houses in plots of a few acres. The policies would probably include modest stabling, a porter's lodge, and sufficient space for a good show of flowers, and a pattern-book conservatory. The outbreak of the First World War was thought to be a watershed, after which life on the Scottish estate would never be the same. An agricultural slump in 1917 further exacerbated the difficulties encountered by estates, and between the wars, a number of great houses were abandoned and demolished. That pattern repeated itself after the Second World War, but the losses were more severe. Many great houses requisitioned by the Army had been so damaged that they had to be demolished thereafter. Some were dynamited, some fired (Panmure), and others used for military target practice (Alva). Since the Scottish rates system levied full rates on a house even if unoccupied, unless it were roofless, many were decapitated. Death duties, and subsequently Capital Transfer Tax seemed to sound an inevitable death-knell for the great estates. Between 1960 and 1973, more than a hundred country houses were demolished.[30]

Yet the demise of the great estate has not yet occurred. It has proved to be surprisingly resilient. Furthermore, despite the grievous losses since 1945, some forty new country houses have been built (although rarely up to the character of those demolished). Although their future is yet again uncertain now that the economy of the local landscape is being determined in Brussels, public opinion has changed to the extent that the contribution these estates make to the economy, landscape and character of Scotland is now appreciated. It is hoped that the tragic losses of the last fifty years may never be repeated.

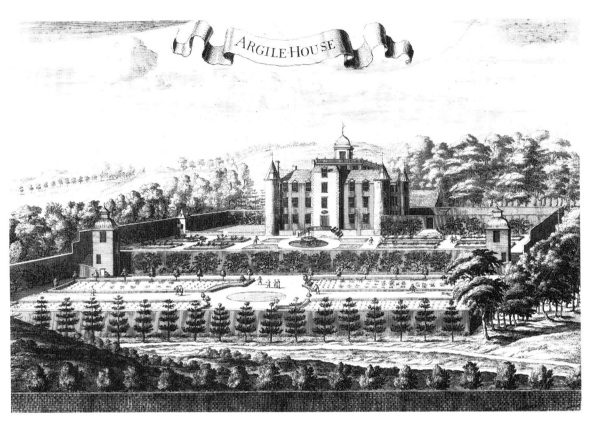

Captain Slezer's view of 'Argile House' actually depicts what was Hatton House until its demolition in the 1960s. High walls shelter the terraced gardens immediately adjacent to the house. In contrast the view of Thirlestane depicts simple formal courts; each side are ranges of service buildings. (Courtesy of the Trustees of the National Library of Scotland.)

24

Chapter 2

Formal Gardens and Planting

A characteristic of the formal European-inspired gardens which the nobility added either to their towers or attracted to their new mansions during the seventeenth century is their proximity to the parent building. Terraces, parterres, knot gardens, banqueting houses, gazebos, flights of steps, and ornamental pools represented an extension of man's civilising influence from the house into the policies beyond. The limit of that influence was defined by walled boundaries, and enhanced by the artificiality of layout and planting within. There was a sharp contrast between these protected pleasure grounds and the untamed—and occasionally dangerous—wildness beyond. Control was always paramount in the design. Large gardens would be divided into several smaller gardens, stepped as necessary, or separated by walls of topiary or boscage. Each section was defined and ordered, and had its role to play in the life of the house.

Captain Slezer's late seventeenth century engravings of Thirlestane, Glamis, and Gordon Castles and Hatton House depict great houses or castles forming part of a single composition with their terraces, gardens, walls, stairs and pavilions. The formality is emphasised by geometric pools with fountains, rows of small trees, low-clipped hedges, espaliers and planted beds.

Terraces

Terraces and parterres might be described as seventeenth century recreation grounds. Whereas the occupants of earlier houses would have exercised in the long gallery within, the occupants of a seventeenth century house would take a formal walk among parterres, or play bowls on the terrace. On appropriate occasions, or at specific times of day, they would repair to some of the buildings encompassed by the walls, each with its specific purpose; perhaps the banqueting house, not for a banquet as we know it now, but for the

25

taking of light refreshment such as syllabub; or the gazebo, for the purpose of looking at the view or (more likely) for the purpose of admiring man's control upon nature; perhaps a bath house; or simply to progress through avenues to dally beside some secluded fountain.

Walled gardens had formed part of the policies of the greater castles, palaces and religious houses since the medieval period. By the sixteenth century, formal gardens and terraces were being added to lesser properties, such as that built for the Earl of Morton at Aberdour in 1572, currently being recreated by Historic Buildings and Monuments. In the seventeenth century, particularly after the Restoration, terraces formed part of what any nobleman aspiring to appear cultivated desired to add to his property. They were sometimes used artificially to heighten the plinth upon which the new house would be built, so as to emphasise its almost defensive command over the surrounding country. Where existing buildings or natural contours rendered artificial terraces unnecessary, slopes and hillsides—preferably tumbling down to a river—were stepped-out accordingly.

One of the most completely recorded terraced gardens is that of the delightful little house at Barncluith, by Hamilton, whose walled gardens, stepping down to the river Avon, were created in the late seventeenth century. In 1729, John Macky enjoyed 'seven hanging Terras walks, down to a riverside, with a wild wood full of birds on the opposite side of the River; in some of those walks are banqueting houses, with walks and grottos, and all of them filled with large evergreens, in the shapes of beasts and birds'.[31] Just under 100 years later, Dorothy Wordsworth was equally enthusiastic noting its yew trees 'cut into fantastic shapes'. She considered it 'one of the most elaborate old things ever seen, a little hanging garden of Babylon'[32]. By 1900, topiary peacocks had been added to yew, holly, acacia, roses and wallflowers and it had trees divided by gravel walks, with a summerhouse to the east, a garden house to the west, a fountain, and the Duke of Hamilton's bath.[33] Sir Robert Lorimer found it 'the most romantic little garden in Scotland . . . four or five terraces, one above the other, sticking on the side of a cliff the general angle of which is about 55°. Two little summerhouses, great trees of scented box. . . .'[34]

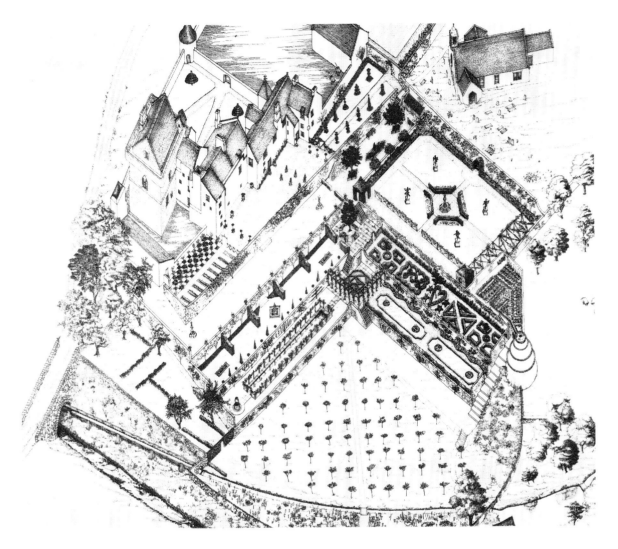

The artificiality of those gardens fell foul of the sweep of the eighteenth century landscapists. Terraces only survived by accident, where money ran out, or where natural contours compelled their survival. Thereafter, the revived terraces in the formal gardens of the nineteenth century were not so much a direct descendant, as a cousin. Gone was the rigid separation from the surrounding landscape, and gone the artificial height. Save at places like Thirlestane, where David Bryce levelled and filled out the great mound upon which the castle stood, edging it with balustrades and steps to make

Aberdour Castle. This bird's-eye view by John Knight shows what may have been there circa 1650, including knot gardens, pavilions, changes in level and, to the bottom right the extant doocot. (Courtesy of Historic Buildings and Monuments.)

27

it appear man-made, terraces were generally lower; only two or three feet above the surrounding countryside, acting as a garden forecourt to the landscape beyond. The garden became an extension of the house and the terrace an outdoor room, with all the additional richness and planting that the Victorians could command. Their edges were much less sharply delineated, with balustrades instead of walls; for, by then, landscapes both within and without the terraces had been equally tamed.

The requirements of what we would now call agribusiness brought a spate of building of a different sort. Some indication of the range of buildings that eventually became necessary for the grandest estates in the nineteenth century can be obtained from a schedule of those that existed within the walled gardens at Dalkeith Palace: vineries, a heath house, tropical plant house, greenhouses, peach houses, north-facing plant house, combined pine stoves and vineries, camelia house, orchid house, fig houses, cherry plum and apricot house, pineapple pits, cucumber pits, propagating pits, cold pits for alpine and greenhouse plants, heated asparagus pit, close-heated sheds for winter forcing of rhubarb and seakale, liquid manure tanks, room for cleaning and arranging vegetables, fruit room, foreman's room, seed room, potting room, carpenter's painter's and glazier's shop, men's room, storerooms, cowhouse, open sheds, washhouse, dairy, gardener's house, summerhouse, stables and lodge. Many were simple lean-to structures against the garden wall, and some clearly had no architectural pretensions whatsoever.[35]

Parterres, Knots and other Gardens

One of the earliest surviving formal gardens is the King's Knot, nestling below the crag of Stirling Castle. Probably laid out in its present form by William Watts, *circa* 1625, when payment is recorded for 'platting and contryveing his Majestie's new orchard and gardein', it consisted of two adjacent gardens whose geometrical pattern of clipped box hedges was punctuated by ornamental trees standing like soldiers.

In 1604, a Renaissance-inspired walled garden was added to the seat of the Lindsays at Edzell Castle, Angus, which survives today

in its celebrated replanted glory. It was a grand gesture by Sir David Lindsay, Lord Edzell to construct this little acre of civilisation at the then boundary of the Highlands; and even grander to incorporate overtly Renaissance motifs in the walls; masons following designs by Albrecht Durer's pupil Meister I. B. of Nürnberg. Save that the castle is now ruined, the ensemble appears not unlike the aspect when first complete, as recorded by a contemporary visitor: 'an excellent dwelling, a great house, delicate gardens with walls sumptuously built of hewn stone polished, with pictures and coats of arms in the walls, with a fyne summerhouse, with a house for a bath on the south corner thereof, far exceeding any new work of their times, excellent kitchine-garden, and orchards of diverse kynds of most excellent fruit, and most delicate new park with fallow-deer'.[36] The occupants of that delicate new park are now rabbits. Clipped box compartments proclaim a motto of the Lind-

Edzell Castle. A restoration of the clipped knot garden best viewed originally from the windows of the first floor Great Hall.

29

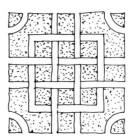

A selection of patterns for laying out parterres with clipped box or a variety of other shrubs or herbs.

says: *Dum Spiro Spero* (While I breathe, I hope). Today, roses lend colour to the compartments, and the blue and white of the family colours are reproduced in flowers, set into the elaborately decorated and carved red sandstone walls. They glow rich and luminously in the evening light.

Parterres

> Around the Fabrik spread the wide Parterre
> Like to a verdant mantle edg'd with Gold
> Or an embroyder'd carpet all perfum'd
> With Indian sweets. . . .
>
> The Country Seat 1727, Sir John Clerk

The treatment of the gardens within the spaces enclosed by the walls and terraces was in formal patterns that probably came to Scotland from the Low Countries and northern Europe. Their patterns display similarities to contemporary design in embroidery and stone carving. Considerable variety was on offer: *parterre a l'angloise, parterre de compartiment*, and *parterre de broderie*. Paths would be formed from a coloured groundwork mixture of sand, charcoal, sifted coal ash, crushed brick, shells and gravel; and these would be used to set off the platted patterns of clipped and richly scented juniper, rosemary, lavender, hyssop, or thyme as alternatives to box.

A Knot Garden is a further elaboration upon a formal garden layout, consisting of a 'conceit' of paths lined with box hedges in the pattern of a knot. Some could be very elaborate, and represented designs less like knots than contemporary strapwork upon buildings.[37]

The great garden at Pitmedden, the largest surviving parterre in Scotland, was designed *circa* 1675 by Alexander Seton, although its current state is a restoration rather than a survival. Overlooked by a raised viewing terrace flanked by twin gazebos (see p 34), the lower garden is reached down a formal flight of stairs. It is arranged round the fountain in four planted rectangles, three of which have been recreated from the 1647 drawing of the parterres at Holyrood by Gordon of Rothiemay. The fourth rectangle acts as a memorial to Alexander Seton, and is planted with his emblem and the inscription clipped in box: *Merces Mae Certa Laborum* (The Sure Reward

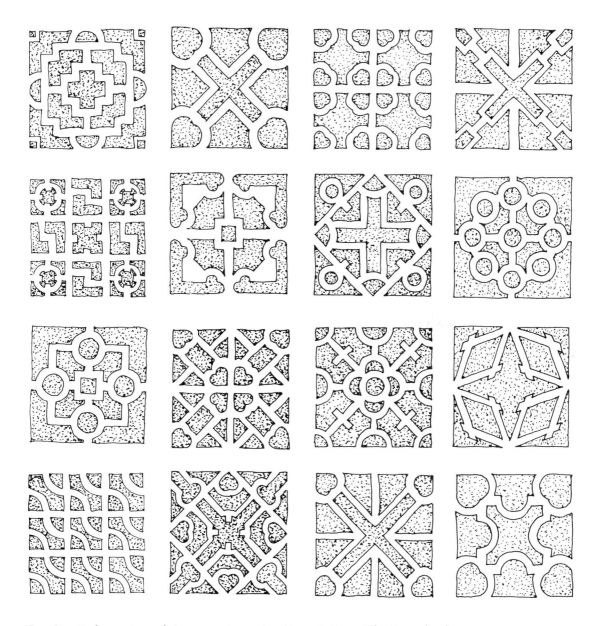

For Our Labours); and *Sustento Sanguine Signa* (I Bear The Standard
With My Blood). The inscriptions commemorate Alexander's
father John, who had first acquired the lands of Pitmedden in 1603,
and died defending the Royal Standard at the Battle of Brig o' Dee
in 1639. His crest can also been seen in the weather-vanes above

31

The Great Garden at Pitmedden was acquired by the NTS in 1952 by which date it had become an overgrown kitchen garden. Restoration carried out 1955-1974 has created the layout seen today. Pitmedden House was destroyed by fire in 1818.

the gazebos. The extent of the parterre, now beautifully maintained by the National Trust for Scotland, is indicated by the fact that 40,000 plants, raised under glass, are planted out each spring, within patterns bordered by some four miles of box hedge. The picture is completed by the normal impedimenta of such a garden—fountains, a sundial and topiary.

The Banqueting House

The 'fine summerhouse' at Edzell was almost certainly a banqueting house, a newly fashionable structure that had become an essential component in new gardens. Its imposing exterior, with suitable gun loops, coped chimneys, and an elaborately corbelled angle turret,

32

bears the impressive monogram of Sir David Lindsay above the main entry door. Windows are leaded lights above ventilating timber shutters, and the roof is of freestone slates. There are two rooms on the ground floor, of which the principal is fitted with a perimeter wall bench of stone, below a ribbed and groined vault. A spiral staircase leads to accommodation above, served by a little closet formed in the angle turret. A 1669 cubic banqueting house survives at Murthly, with an ogee roof capped by a 1775 weather-vane. A pavilion at Dunrobin Castle, dated 1723, was also probably used as a banqueting house. Recently restored by Benjamin Tindall, this building lies just outside the walled garden and forms part of a larger structure, fronted with a stone staircase and a large brick extension to the rear.

The garden pavilion at Murthly, a retreat for supping flummeries and trifles, built into the inside of the enclosing garden wall.

33

The Gazebo

The joy of the gazebo is that its name is probably a spoof; the origin of the word, by analogy with lavabo (a place where one washes) is that a gazebo is a place from which one gazes. It is thus an ornamental turret. Gazebos form part of formal garden design, usually built in pairs flanking and terminating the terrace overlooking gardens below, and sometimes joined to them by a staircase. Gazebos generally take the form of a cube or double cube, with an ogee roof. The seventeenth century gazebos at Pitmedden are very grand exemplars of the period; two-storey structures with slated ogee roofs, larger and squatter than many, their lower storeys being vaulted with four ribs and a boss, and entered from the garden. Their original use was probably as a garden shed (or bath house). The principal rooms upstairs are entered from the terrace, and consist of an inviting, vaulted viewing gallery, with a warm-red paved floor, bolection-moulded fireplace, and wood panelling with paintings in wall recesses. The Pitmedden gazebos are similar in both date and design to those at Hatton and Traquair.[38] The 1697 gazebos at Melville House are rather different, linked by a low screen wall which featured lead statues of Mercury and Fame on central gate piers. They terminated the view along a half-mile long beech avenue.

Smaller, circular gazebos survive in the gardens at Meldrum and Cockenzie. The former, inset into an earth bank below the house, have latticed doors at first-floor level which presumably led onto a balcony which no longer exists. Those at Cockenzie are no more than ornamental turrets, offering a glimpse over a small garden from below a steeply pointed conical hat. The accommodation is so limited, hardly more than standing room, that its erection may have been largely symbolic.

Gazebos also fell before the free-flowing landscapists of the eighteenth century, and were revived again in the nineteenth as an adjunct to terraces. Of the new type of gazebo, examples by Rowand Anderson at Pollok House, Glasgow, survive as part of a complex of terraces, fountains and planting, with lions and urns sculptured by Hew Lorimer. The most elaborate of the later gazebos can be found at Torosay Castle, Mull, joined by a heavily buttressed wall

The twin gazebos at Melville are dated 1697; they terminated the approach avenue just in front of the house.

planted with mimosa and jasmine overlooking the Fountain and Lion Terraces. These exuberant pavilions, rising to crenellated parapets below pyramid roofs are vigorously decorated with bull's-eye windows and ball finials. Cantilevered stone stairs, finished with Italianate balusters, complete the composition.

Some twentieth century gazebos were built for new and revived gardens. The 1907 Italian Garden at Glamis, bounded by a high hedge of yew, contains twin open-work gazebos in seventeenth century style, one displaying a commemorative stone celebrating the craftsman and the local people who were involved in the project. A similar re-creation took place, at about the same time, when the derelict garden at Kinross was reborn, involving the construction of small pavilions and a loggia. As at Glamis, there is a commemorative plaque.

Working Gardens

In the foreground of Slezer's view of Culross Abbey House is a separate, walled kitchen garden. So was there also, it seems, in the new gardens at Aberdour. Bishop Pococke's description of Blair Atholl, some seventy years later, gives an indication of just how grand such 'kitchen gardens' could become:

> in the whole length of which the Kitchen garden, the Duke has made a fine piece of water, with six or seven islands and penin-sulars in it, two of which are for swans to breed on, having that-ched houses built on them for that purpose, and the wild ducks breed on the islands: the Garden is formed in a gentle declivity on each side and all walled round. There is a pidgeon house at one Angle, and a Gardener's house at another, and at the south end is a semi-circular Summer house which is all glass in the front: in the walk leading to this, and on each side of the Cross Walk, are about twenty grotesque figures in lead, and painted, which have a pretty effect in that situation, at each end is a parterre of many sorts of perennial flowers . . . This is the most beautiful Kitchen garden I believe in the world.[39]

All that remains is a ruinous Chinese bridge, and a curious little nineteenth century pavilion with an ogee roof built into the garden wall as a showpiece for hunting trophies.

Formal layouts adjacent to the house were anathema to the land-scapist of the eighteenth century, who desired houses to appear as villas in parkland, and took a particular dislike to anything so overtly primitive as a working garden. It offended both eye and nostril, as John Reid had forecast in his pioneering influential tome *The Scots Gardiner* which he published in 1683.[40] He recommended that a walled garden be best located near stables, 'out of sight of the front

of the house . . . the impropriety of the view to see dung in that garden, . . . for eyes should be more agreeably entertained by lawns, avenues and vistas'. Working gardens were banished to a distance and remained there for something over a 100 years, until fashion reverted. In 1829 William Cobbett was representing a widespread view when he wrote 'It is a most miserable taste to seek to poke away the kitchen garden, in order to get it out of sight. If well managed, nothing is more beautiful'.[41]

Formal Gardens

As formal gardens and terraces recovered popularity in the nineteenth century, many seventeenth century designs were reconstructed—exemplified by the Drumlanrig Gardens, restored with its parterres by Charles McIntosh, the Duke of Buccleuch's head gardener. At Abbotsford, Sir Walter Scott rejected the notion of the villa in parkland, and provided adjacent to the house formal gardens

Built into a viewing terrace above the level of the parterre, the twin gazebos at Pitmedden have undergone considerable restoration since their construction in the late seventeenth century. The ogee roofs are quite recent and internal panelling was brought from a contemporary property in Midlothian.

At Torosay the gazebos are very fine examples, with exuberant details – such as the cantilevered staircases – not usually associated with such structures.

divided into courts by means of turreted walls, gates, and an open work masonry screen based upon the structures in Melrose Abbey, decorated with little carved bosses. The new fashion caught on. In 1826, William Burn and W. S. Gilpin began the restoration of Sir William Bruce's simple terraces at Balcaskie, and in 1844 W. A. Nesfield added decorative gateways, grand hanging staircases leading from the original gardens down to new lawns, and a new bowling green flanked by parterres. The gardens were specifically designed to frame the axial view from the house south to the Bass Rock in the Forth. It is said that the Rock appears to move upstream or downstream according to local weather conditions.

One of the earliest, and certainly the grandest of the nineteenth century formal gardens open to the public, is the thirteen acre garden at Drummond Castle near Crieff. Begun in 1789 by George Kennedy, it was so developed between 1820 and 1840 by Louis Kennedy in association with the celebrated theorist J. C. Loudon, that it became famous far beyond Scotland. A new drive up to the castle, completed in 1842, quite possibly for Queen Victoria's visit, now serves to bring the visitor unawares upon what was clearly designed to be a viewing platform. A fabulous spectacle is laid out below, comprising geometrically designed gravel paths and grass walks, bordered with flowers and hedges brought into focus by a Saltire (or St Andrew's Cross) plan. Its key points are occupied by architectural features, such as the 1630 sundial from the original garden, an early nineteenth century statue of Jupiter, and a number of white Italian marble statues and vases. Two large, circular parterres are enclosed by topiary yews and holly trees, studded with conical cypresses and pleached purple plum trees.

The fashion now re-established, formal gardens appear frequently, albeit different from their seventeenth century cousins. Sir Reginald Blomfield's 1909 Italianate garden at Mellerstain forms a delightful podium for a garden party; balustraded terrace walls are punctuated with fine stone urns which are decorated with horned rams' heads. Plats of lavender and rosebeds among greenery are clipped into starburst shapes and set amidst hexagonal planting beds. The main view across the lake focuses on the distant silhouette of the Hundy Mundy, a castellated uninhabitable folly with a rubble-built facade.

38

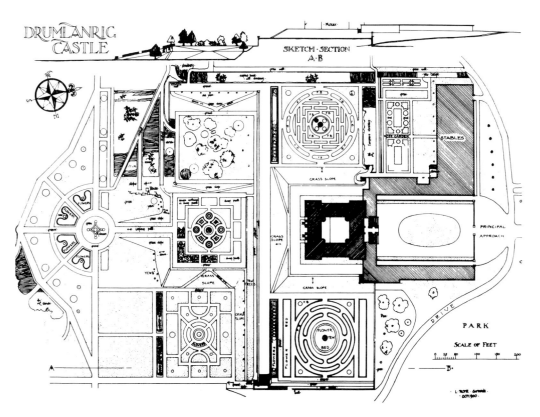

Plan of Drumlanrig gardens from H I Triggs' book 'Formal Gardens in England and Scotland' published in 1902. It shows a wide range of patterns for bedding-out interspersed with gravel walks and yew trees. (Courtesy of the Trustees of the National Library of Scotland.)

Victorian designs for parterre and labyrinth formed from clipped shrubs probably emphasised with bright flowers and hard edgings.

Abbotsford is built into a series of enclosures with walls which range in style from the quasi-medieval with turrets, to an openwork screen. Each court has its own character, emphasised with carvings and statuary.

What kinds of Flowers?

Early gardens were cultivated entirely for their medicinal qualities, any decorative effects being a by-product. Since imported decorative flowers remained expensive even to the late seventeenth century,[42] it seems unlikely that there would have been much elaborate flower planting in Scotland, certainly before the foundation of the Botanic Gardens in Edinburgh in 1670, by Sir Robert Sibbald, author of the influential *Scotia Illustrata*. The Earl of Breadalbane's accounts for Taymouth the following year imply that expenditure upon decorative flowers and bushes was becoming a significant factor; for they included provision for 100 honeysuckle, 50 laburnum, 30 monthly roses, and 25 rose standards.[43] These new varieties were used to supplement native stock—plants largely the descendants of those used in medieval physic gardens,—such as

violet, heliotrope, mandrake, borage, poppies, cornflowers, fox-gloves, daffodils and gentians. The new fashion for something more exotic created a demand for seeds. Seed catalogues were certainly in use by the time of the publication of Reid's *The Scots Gardiner* in 1683, since it describes a garden laid out specifically for decorative flowers: a chequerboard of crocus, anemone, cowslip, boar's ear, gilly flower, carnations and a few tulips—nothing hugely experimental.

Even at the two houses Sir William Bruce built for himself—Balcaskie (1665), and Kinross (1684–1693), properties with some of the most elaborate gardens of their day, the flowers seem to have been limited to narcissus, lily, hyacinth and double jonquils (all imported from Europe for the purpose). Later editions of *The Scots Gardiner* describe walks laid out with pots of carnations and myrtle,

The Italianate Garden at Drummond viewed from the terrace – a spectacular panorama.

41

The terrace at Manderston
forms an outside room from
which to view the landscaped
grounds.

The terrace at Manderston forms an outside room from which to view the landscaped grounds.

musk roses, eglantines and yellow briars. By 1730, garden flowers in regular use in large Scottish gardens included madonna lily, clove carnations, mullein, lupin, red primrose, polyanthus, guelder rose, pink geranium, scarlet lychnis, anemone, convolvulus, sunflower, sweet william, scabious, hyacinth, moss rose and canterbury bells.[44]

The gardening palette broadened with the introduction of dahlias by Lady Bute in 1789, and varieties of zinnia and campanula in the 1790s. 'Scotch Roses' were first bred in Perth in 1802. Over the next thirty years, the introduction of further foreign species accelerated: of the 150 varieties of flower seed advertised in the *Floricultural Cabinet*, in 1836, seventy-four—including petunia and eschscholtzia—were recent introductions from the Americas. In his celebrated book *The Flower Garden*, Charles McIntosh identified the most popular garden flowers of 1840: many tulips, dahlias, roses, pansies, carnations, ranunculus and hyacinth. Plant collecting expeditions to China and the Himalayas added further exotica to

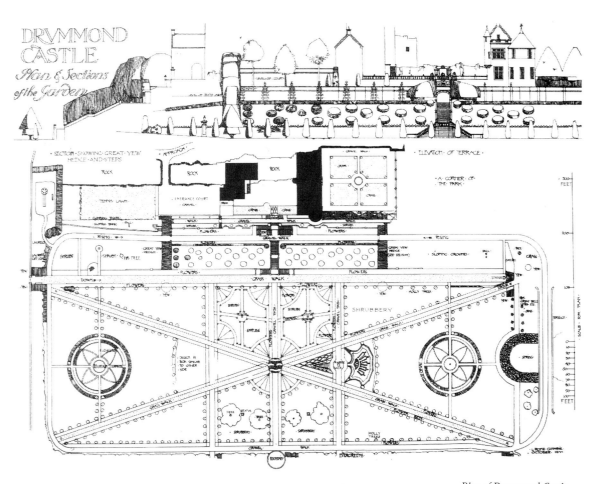

Plan of Drummond Castle gardens by H I Triggs dated 1900 shows clearly the Saltire layout with Mylne's sundial at its centre, on axis with symmetrical statues. The section gives some idea of the elevation of the castle building above the garden, essential to view such a layout successfully. (Courtesy of the Trustees of the National Library of Scotland.)

The Hundy Mundy at Mellerstain offers no shelter, being a purely ornamental two-dimensional screen best viewed from afar.

the gardener's repertory: particularly azalias, rhododendrons, and camelias. Some of the finest present-day rhododendron collections, for example, that at Stonefield Castle in Argyll, contain plants directly linked to those expeditions.

The Walled Garden

The long tradition of controlled fruit cultivation in Scotland implies that the earliest detached, walled gardens may have been orchards. One was recorded in 1524 at Ballencrief, and another was added to Megginch Castle in 1575. Indeed, *Scotia Illustrata* listed more than 400 species of plant and fruit trees then in cultivation in Scotland.[45]

It is doubtful that orchards comprised a specific building type. John Reid recommended that a single garden be divided into separate sections, for herbs, fruit, flowers and vegetables—in patches demarcated by low hedges of box, currant, gooseberry and dwarf trees. Paths were to be edged with parsley, violets, strawberries or gilly flowers. Reid aimed to produce 'a garden for pleasure', and that for which he was responsible at Aberdour had a formal walled garden, terraces, parterres, a kitchen garden and an orchard. In 1687, in order to increase the variety of the garden, he ordered seeds of plums, cherries, tamarisks, figs, gooseberries, raspberries, jasmine and almonds from the Physic Garden in Edinburgh.[46]

Visiting old Culzean Castle in 1692, William Abercrummie observed 'very pretty gardens and orchards, adorned with excellent terraces, the walls loaded with peaches, apricots, cherries and other fruits; and these gardens are so well sheltered from the north and east winds and lie so open to the south, that the fruits and herbage are more early than any other place in Carrick'. By 1733, the terraced walls of Brechin Castle had, according to contemporary description, growing against them 'quince, old pippin, black mulberryie, English pergamon, May cherry, Algier apprecok, Roman red, nectarin, Newington peach, blew primordian, great blew fige, honeysuckle, apprecok, orgelen, old apprecok, Violet Hasting peach, almond, old apprecok, old blue primordian plumbe, old plum, and Hampden's bergamond'[47] among other exotic fruits. In the same decade, the new gardens surrounding Panmure contained

espaliers laden with apricots, peaches, nectarines, figs, plums, almonds, quince and cherries.[48]

Early free-standing walled gardens were generally square or rectangular in plan. John Reid discouraged semi-circular plans 'most erroneously practiced, for there the wind, being pended up, occasions squirls and retards the ripening of the fruit there planted'. A southerly aspect was recommended, on sloping land to encourage drainage. Wind breaks of fir plantations were suggested for the north, east and west. A two-acre garden might support a small family, whereas six to eight acres were recommended for larger establishments. If additional walls for training fruit trees were needed, larger gardens could be, and were, subdivided into sections.

The 1739 brick-lined garden at Mavisbank, just south of Edinburgh, was modelled on the Colosseum: 'a great circle, walled in the bottom of a steep valley, surrounded by a fine, rapid river, that gives

The Fish Gate at Kinross carries the view from the house across Loch Leven. The gatepier finials depict boys astride dolphins.

45

a most beautiful prospect to the house and gardens above it'.[49] By contrast, a 1740 walled garden at Netherbyres is elliptical in shape; that at Fingask eight-sided, semi-quatrefoil both at Drumoak and Park House. The Brechin Castle garden, cinquefoil in plan and of enormous extent, is enclosed by walls nearly five metres high. Within can be found topiary, statuary, glasshouses, sundials, a pair of columns, and a gardener's house. The horseshoe shaped walled garden at Guthrie Castle includes a fine east gate, a Gothick garden house, a whale jaw-bone arch, and a Doric portico surmounted by a carved stone inscribed 'WG 1614'.

Walled gardens rose in visual importance in the eighteenth century, and began to fulfil a processional and ceremonial role. They were a demonstration of the foresight of the landowner, and some-times of his wealth—as some of them grew to considerable size (for instance the walled garden at Inveraray has rubble walls over 150 metres long, in places over six metres tall). These new architectural gardens required care. That at Penicuik, built pre 1730 (against John Reid's advice to an unusual D plan), contains the charming two-storey pavilion of Eskfield, a classical essay in brick, with round-headed windows, stone dressings and pedimented gable. A good example of the array of buildings that eventually became attached to walled gardens can be seen at the Culzean walled garden, where you can find sundials, greenhouses, a collection of palm trees, a Swiss cottage, the gardener's house, and a Victorian grotto.

Noted gardeners, who could almost be considered as landscape gardeners, were involved in their design: William Bowie at Duff House, Banff, Walter Nicol at Invermay, and John Hay, at Camper-down Park, Dundee. James Bowie was responsible for the classical garden added to Redhall House, Edinburgh, in 1758. John Hender-son was responsible for a particularly memorable garden at Amisfield, 1783, which enclosed some 4,000 square metres with walls of gaunt dressed stone blocks, distinguished by four enormous cylindrical corner pavilions. Each pavilion presents a severe six-column portico to the garden, with a panel of decorative scagliola above the doorway. They were once crowned with classical cupolas, one of which doubled as a doocot. The garden at Luffness, near North Berwick, is unique in that a second set of walls enclose an inner garden—a *jardin clos*; this diamond plan inner sanctum was designed to shelter French pear trees with greengages at the centre.

The Garden Gate

Gateways mark transition from one zone to another, and are both functionally and symbolically important. The seventeenth century Fish Gate at Kinross forms part of a larger walled composition that now includes pavilions and loggias. Gates are frequently named after either their design or their statuary. Thus there is a Swan Gate at Keir dominated by a swan, wings reared up, head down low at the end of a long curving neck. The 'Chinese Moon Gate' at Leith Hall takes the form of a completely circular opening in a rubble garden wall, which concentrates strong sunshine into a lovely pool of light. Marble figures depicting the four seasons cap the gate piers at Manderston, and it has been said that these gates were gilded to pick out the glow of the evening sun. A curious gateway inserted into the walled garden at Preston Hall has many elaborate stones and buttress finials depicting heraldic animals. The 1838 gate to the kitchen garden at Taymouth takes the same form as the gate to the entire park: a perpendicular Gothick arch with sprocketed finials, which now opens to a prestige development of holiday homes in the garden. When the original rubble-built garden at Penicuik was regarded as inadequate in 1870, the new red-brick garden created some distance away, was given crested iron gates, hung on masonry piers. The lower part of each gate is decorated with a cast lion's head. Above, set into the overthrow, is an armorial shield and a figure, horn to mouth, proclaiming 'Free for a Blast', a motto of the Clerk family.

Buildings in Walled Gardens

Built structures had been integral to the formal terraced gardens of the seventeenth and early eighteenth centuries, and continued to be once gardens became detached and distanced from the houses they served. Walled gardens retain a variety of pavilions, apple houses, growing houses, conservatories, orangeries and gardener's houses. Among the earliest of such structures is the apple house. Usually simple pyramid-roofed, two-storey structures built into one corner

of the garden wall, the ground floor, as with gazebos, was usually entered from within the garden, while steps leading up the outside face led to accommodation, possibly for the gardener, at first floor level. Good examples may be found at Johnstounburn and at the Old House, Belhaven.

The twin octagonal pavilions built in 1795 at Preston Hall, near Edinburgh, are among the most pleasant garden pavilions in Scotland. Brick, with freestone dressings and pediments over the windows, they are built into the wall that sub-divides the garden. One pavilion contains an elegant staircase and the other, linked to it by a catwalk, acts as a "fruit room, tea-room, library or small horticultural museum". Rooftop weather-vanes project into the ceilings below to inform those inside as to the state of the weather. The greenhouses pitched against the catwalk earned the displeasure of J. C. Loudon: 'The modern method of carrying summer houses

Yester. The gardener's house with its gothick facade of red sandstone forms a dramatic focus to views right across the walled garden.

Opposite
The Pineapple at Dunmore, rescued from dereliction, is now let for short holidays. (Royal Commission on Ancient Monuments, Scotland.)

49

above hot houses as at Preston Hall . . . has a very bad effect on scenery, besides their incongruity, when considered as overlooking the kitchen garden which certainly, like the kitchen itself, is not an object intended for beauty'.[50]

The construction of garden pavilions was rather a matter of whim on the part of the owner, and their quality came to be a test of his discernment and wealth. There are fine examples at Arbuthnott, Arthurstone and Blair Adam, but undoubtedly the most extraordinary pavilion built in the eighteenth century is the 1761 Pineapple at Dunmore, by Airth, set into an enormous six-acre walled garden at some distance from the ruined house and old tower. The garden was so elaborate that the walls were honeycombed with flues for furnaces behind, (chimneys disguised as large stone vases) with stone bothies constructed for the gardeners and their assistants. The extraordinary Pineapple pavilion is the focus of the north wall. Its Palladian porch leads from the garden through a passage and out again to steps which lead up to a Gothick room lit by ogee-headed windows, adorned with leaf carvings. Leaves of the pineapple spread out above in magnificent freestone, each one drained internally to avoid frost damage. Above the leaves, the dome carries on in stone pineapple form to its apex. It is said that this magnificent piece of eccentricity was built for the twenty-nine-year-old Earl of Dunmore, later Governor of New York.

The Gardener's House

Although gardeners must have been valued from earliest times, the arrival of new plants, seed catalogues and landlord ambition in the seventeenth century led to the employment of the expert gardener, and of the necessity of providing him with a house. It is of some significance, that in 1695, George Burne agreed to work at Taymouth as gardener for the Earl of Breadalbane at an annual wage of £15— no mean salary at that date.[51] The Taymouth estate eventually provided a gardener's house, complete with kitchen, parlour and "high east room" which contained a bed with blue curtains, and garret.[52] When the Grants of Monymusk sought a new gardener in 1755, they expected the successful applicant to be conversant in all aspects

Built into the longest of the walls which comprise the enormous walled garden at Gordon Castle are the frontages of two houses. It has been suggested that this one was a Dower House.

The house of the Head Gardener at Manderston is a grand example dated 1897, the entry court dominated by a sundial.

of horticulture, including knowledge of hothouses; for its part, the estate undertook to provide him with the necessary instruments, tools and books.[53]

The head gardener came to assume a position of considerable responsibility in large estates, and his house was sufficiently attractive and important to enhance a tour of the policies. Occasionally it doubled as a principal lodge, but more often, it was linked to the walled garden and sometimes contained a horticultural library. That at Yester is at the far end of the garden, axially facing entrance gates of Art Nouveau ironwork. It has a Gothick façade of glowing red ashlar stone, with three pointed-arch windows, and two recessed square niches displaying statuary. Lean-to glasshouses below are screened behind espaliers and a row of statues upon pedestals. Two-storey gardeners' houses can be found built into the garden walls at Darleith, Ballimore, and Culzean. Each contains windows facing both inward to the garden and outward to the estate beyond. A particularly luxurious freestanding example of baronial style was built in 1897 at Manderston, with its own planted courtyard, and an ornate sundial at the centre.

Conservatories and Orangeries

Such fruit as was stored in the seventeenth century and earlier, was stored in a 'fruitery', or 'conservatory'—at this date implying a simple pavilion like an apple house in the corner of the garden. One hundred and fifty years later, the meaning of the word conservatory had changed. From being a building storing picked fruits, it had become one designed for the protection, cultivation and nourishment of living, and often exotic, plants. The purpose of conservatories and orangeries was fundamentally similar: to provide a light, sheltered space with controlled temperatures and ventilation for the propagation of flowers, fruit and plants. The architectural distinction, if there is one, lies in the fact that orangeries were usually designed in a formal relationship to the house, and thus nearly always of masonry construction; whereas the design of conservatories was controlled by material, components, and erection techniques. Differences in the way the two buildings were used were matters of degree rather than of kind. Both performed a hor-

Beanston Orangery, located just outside the walled garden, is one of the earliest examples of such a building to survive in Scotland.

William Burn's design dated 1831 for the conservatory at Dalkeith Palace which was described as 'the most elaborate . . . in the kingdom'. (Royal Commission on Ancient Monuments, Scotland.)

ticultural function, and both offered the opportunity of a formal extension to the facilities and activities of the house. As orangeries became more picturesque, so did conservatories. As they began to contain aviaries and ponds, so did conservatories. As functional plants were eventually moved out of orangeries to make way for decorative plants, so were they also in conservatories.

The 1704 Orangery at Kensington Palace, London, was probably the first purpose built example of its kind in Britain. Alternative experiments began with temporary versions which were dismantled in summer, followed by orange houses on rollers. Eventually, it was concluded that the best solution was a long building with tall, south-facing sash windows, with straw insulation, shutters, and a back wall heated with a stove. An extravagant orangery would, in addition to containing orange and lemon trees, be host to bergamot, myrtle and pomegranates; all planted into tubs which could be moved out on to the terrace when required. Few were built in Scotland, and one of the even fewer to survive is the modest structure at Beanston, built *circa* 1760, and located beside the walled garden. It is a plain, tall stone building with four huge arched windows. Larger, more sophisticated nineteenth century orangeries can be found at Culzean, Gordon Castle, and Arniston, designed less for cultivation than as an appropriate location for summer fêtes and tea dances.

The history of the conservatory follows that of technology, particularly the technology of steam heating. J. C. Loudon dated the arrival of steam heat in Scotland as early as 1755; but it seems not to have become at all common until the early nineteenth century. The grander conservatories of the late eighteenth century shared common characteristics with the orangery. One was built in 1798 at Wemyss Castle with a freestone façade decorated with Corinthian pilasters and circular windows; and a similarly ambitious structure, with masonry walls supporting a hipped, glazed roof, was built by Sir Walter Scott in the walled garden at Abbotsford in 1820.[54] The majority of more ordinary glasshouses, set against garden walls, were heated by the decomposition of vegetable matter in specially designed pits; and by the hot rear walls hollowed out with flues. Heat loss at night proved to be a problem, but was minimised by pulling down curtains of coarse woollen cloth. In

1792, a Mr Mawer of Dalry, Edinburgh, contrived to heat three pineries, two vineries and two peach houses with steam admitted directly to the air of the glass house, and allowed to condense on the plants themselves. It was a complicated method, and was eventually replaced by the piped hot water greenhouse, the first of which in Scotland was probably that installed at Dalkeith Palace in 1832.

It was installed in possibly the most elaborate of all architectural conservatories, designed for the Duchess of Buccleuch by William Burn. This remarkable, circular, free-standing building was intended to be set at the centre of a formal parterre. It was built of a fine, white sandstone carved into strapwork, which framed the double-thick glazing, unfortunately, all now gone. Its eminence was increased by being raised above a semi-underground cellar, which contained furnaces, boilers, storage for coal, ashes and mould (and was a suitable location for potting plants, growing mushrooms, and for storing rainwater collected from the roof, piped down through two of the pilasters). A central elaborate chimney supported the iron trusses of the roof structure. The Duke of Buccleuch's erudite head gardener Charles McIntosh described it as 'the most elaborate and probably the best specimen of a truly architectural conservatory in the kingdom . . . for elaborate workmanship and eloquence of design, this house as an architectural conservatory is not equalled by any we have seen, nor is there perhaps in Britain a finer specimen'.[55]

The abolition of the glass tax in 1845 was celebrated in the glass pavilions of the 1851 Great Exhibition. From now onwards, the proportion of glass would increase, and that of masonry would diminish. The development of prefabricated cast iron and glass made conservatories much more widely available, and the fact that the glass could be used to hold rigid the metal frame lent itself to the creation of wonderfully curved shapes. One of the most spectacular results is the Kibble Palace in Glasgow's Botanic Gardens. Originally built for his house at Coulport by John Kibble, a colourfully eccentric botanist, astronomer and photographer, the Palace was relocated to Glasgow in 1872. Its double-bellying glass is almost oriental in form, and the largest dome has a circumference of four hundred and seventy-one feet, supported on thirty six iron columns.

At Culzean, the Camellia House is a freestanding gothick pavilion no longer glazed. It dates from 1818.

Amid the delicate scent and warm colours of camellia, bougain-villaea and other exotic plants can be found bleached white marble statues, one of which is King Robert of Sicily seated with a monkey on his arm.

Conservatories were modified for the specialist requirements of particular plants. The camellia being susceptible to damage from excessive sunlight required a camellia house; which was a conservatory with restricted glazing at roof level. The popularity of the gigantic lily *Victoria regia* of the 1851 Great Exhibition led to another variation—the glazed lily enclosure, which was not unlike a marine garden or aquarium. It was a glass house erected over a vase-shaped basin of water, with a fountain at the centre. Usually there would be a vault below for furnace and cold store. Miniature versions were to be found in the vestibules of many larger houses; but, as usual, the proposals for that at Dalkeith Palace were of an

56

imperialist grandeur. The Dalkeith lily enclosure was to have been free-standing, circular, and covered with a shallow glazed roof. A horizontal wheel below water level, kept in motion by a small jet of water, would give the effect of ripples like a river. It is unclear whether this extraordinary device was ever completed.

Other exotic species bred their own enclosures. Patrick Allan Fraser added a new Fernery to his walled garden at Hospitalfield, *circa* 1870. Its purpose was to enclose tropical ferns, plants and trees. A simple stone square with a glazed roof, it was steam-heated from beneath. Access was by means of a perforated terrazzo walkway.

Topiary

Topiary, the clipping into artificial shapes of bushes like yew, holly and hawthorn, was probably introduced to Britain from Holland in the late fifteenth century, but records for it are scarce before the seventeenth. In his volume *A New Orchard and Garden* published in 1618, William Lawson exhorted landowners: 'Your gardner can frame your lesser wood to the shape of men armed in the field, ready to give battle; of swift-running Grey hounds, or of well scented and true-running Hounds to chase the Deer, or hunt the Hare. This kind of hunting shall not waste your Corn, nor much your coyne!'[56] The appeal of a cheap, evergreen and obedient army must have appealed to the Scots mentality. It caught on. Evergreen squares of holly, some forty feet high, were formed at Colinton House, Edinburgh, as an enclosure for 4,500 plants. Alexander Edward's proposals for gardens at Kinnaird Castle in 1695, included the design for a bowling green which was detailed with indications of flower borders, statues, shrubs and possibly topiary: it would not have been unusual.

Sometimes topiary was also used to commemorate a great event, that being the reason for the yews planted at Malleny House, Edinburgh, to commemorate the 1707 Act of Union. But it was a late example. Fashion was moving away from artificiality. In 1708, Alexander Edward was involved in making great plans for the parkland at Hamilton, which included the sweeping away of the old walled gardens around the palace and their replacement with a series of orchards, labyrinths and groves. In 1713, Alexander Pope

Patterns for topiary showing just a few possibilities.

57

View of topiary at Fingask photographed circa 1905. (Royal Commission on Ancient Monuments, Scotland.)

ridiculed 'Adam and Eve in yew, Adam a little shatter'd by the fall of the Tree of Knowledge in the Great Storm: Eve and the Serpent . . . very flourishing: . . . a lavender pig with sage growing in his belly: . . . St George in box, his arms scarce long enough, but will be in condition to stick the dragon by next April'.[57] After Waterloo, and with the revival in interest of formal gardens, fashion changed back. The owners of Coltness and Airlie Castles established topiary layouts representing the positions of army formation in battle; and in a large number of other gardens were created a formidable array of clipped shapes. They ranged from simple cubes, pyramids and obelisks, to spirals and spheres round as huge surreal billiard balls by the green baize of a bowling green. In 1887, Lady Drummond

58

created a topiary crown of green and golden yew at Megginch to celebrate Queen Victoria's jubilee. Fifty topiary sculptures adorn the south lawn at Fingask, and a further 250 conical yews are set out amid nineteenth century garden statues. As part of Sir Robert Lorimer's garden designs at Earlshall, the yews were clipped into the forms of huge chess pieces.

Topiary at Earlshall. It is rumoured that Lorimer arranged for the yews to be brought from a neglected garden in Edinburgh, paying a tip for each plant which survived the trip; they all did!

Boscage

Boscage is the architectural use of great walls of foliage to subdivide gardens, and create tunnels and buttresses. Sometimes this living architecture was decorated with songbirds in cages. Good examples

59

can be seen in the garden of the Hill of Tarvit (National Trust for Scotland), and at Balcaskie. The walled garden at Guthrie Castle is divided by boscage into a central roundel, a radiating avenue, and two arms. Dark greenery of dense foliage against the garden walls at Abbotsford is cut away to reveal a set of five medallions from the old Mercat Cross of Edinburgh presented to Sir Walter Scott by Henry Raeburn in 1822. Similar greenery enhances white Italianate statues at Tyninghame, while boscage is used at Crathes to subdivide the pleasure garden into a series of intimate and thematic shelters—including the Colour Garden, the Golden Garden, and the Fountain Garden.[58]

The Wilderness

John, sixth Earl of Mar, was credited by the Earl of Haddington as the man who introduced the 'Wilderness way of planting' at his Palace of Alloa before 1714. But what did it mean? John Reid considered that 'as it is only for shade and ornament, it is laid out in what figure the owner pleases, there can be no rule given'. In essence, a Wilderness was an artificial woodland designed to incorporate rushing streams, groves, leafy tunnels, pleached alleyways and bird song. Occasionally there would be provision for vegetables, bee skeps, and bogus graves of philosophers to heighten atmosphere. Focal points would be identified by statues and temples.[59] Until the mid eighteenth century, Wilderness design was marked by reluctance to move away from axial vistas and rigidly geometric walks. It is exemplified by the 1726 Wilderness at Arniston, which consisted of woods intersected by alleys bordered by yew hedges. The main feature was a cascade formed at very great expense by diverting two burns into a reservoir. At dinner time, the water was let off as a spectacle and ran for about an hour.

Arboreta and Pineta

The descendant of the Wilderness in the nineteenth century became a specialist collection of trees, called the arboretum or pinetum; and the link between the two was underlined by the laying out of the 1850 pinetum at Blair over part of the original 1737 Wilderness of Diana's Grove.

Raw material for these horticultural experiments were exotic trees and bushes discovered in the New World, or sent home by immigrants. They were first cautiously cossetted under glass, then laid out in avenues in an analytical way, according either to place of origin, or botanical name. The Scone pinetum, laid out in 1848, contains thirty-seven different species of conifer, all planted within its first twelve years of existence. It is one of the finest collections of rare conifers in Britain. However, a better understanding of the characteristics of the new plants and trees soon led to their being planted in a more relaxed way, so that they blended with and complemented the existing vegetation; and thus the fashion faded.[60]

View from near the top of Crathes Castle overlooking the gardens which are subdivided by great walls of boscage which date from 1702. In the far corner sits the doocot, moved to its present position in 1935.

Design dated 1728 by Sir John Clerk for a cascade at Drumlanrig Castle. The remains of a cascade in the castle policies are said to be the subject of a curse. (Courtesy of Sir John Clerk of Penicuik.)

Design

The Victorians were eclectic: that is to say, they would use and transform any influence that took their fancy. They were inclusive

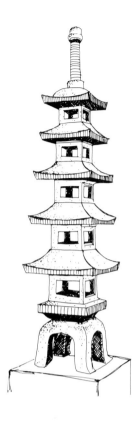

Lakeside Japanese lantern at Manderston House.

rather than exclusive people, and placed no value judgment upon having a variety of approaches to garden design. In 1853, Charles McIntosh distinguished four principal styles. The first was *formal*, or geometric which included vegetable sculpture or topiary in architectural gardens with steps, parapets, basins and terraces—an amended revival of the seventeenth century formal garden. The second was *informal* or picturesque, with fountains and statues, terraced Italian gardens, layouts in the Dutch style with canals, and earth mounds enhancing a flat terrain. This category was divided into 'refined', 'trivial', and 'rough' – the last seemingly in imitation of a Highland glen. The third style was *mixed* – apparently a mixture of the previous two with added architectural elements and viewing points. The fourth was *revivalist*, which meant what it said: layouts called panopticon, Florentine or even Elizabethan; and plants and shrubs chosen for scent as much as colour – peppermint, musk rose and thyme. These styles were all made possible by acres of greenhouses, armies of gardeners, and troops of bedding plants.

In the late nineteenth century, fashion reacted against the mosaic culture of massed flower beds, and moved towards either the new herbaceous border, proselytised by Gertrude Jekyll, or specialist collections such as woodland or alpine gardens. They seemed to have generated no particular building type or form of their own. The brief twentieth century flirtation with Japanese gardens brought to Scotland oriental dragons and lions, complemented at Dalzell, near Hamilton with steps modelled on those of a temple in Nagasaki.[61] The gardens at Carnell included a pagoda, Japanese lanterns and Burmese Chinths. At Stobo Hylton Philipson created three lakes, the lower two linked by cascades and rills in a Japanese manner. The most complete oriental garden, however, was that created at Cowden, near Alloa, by the explorer Ella Christie and her Japanese gardener Taki Honda, advised by Professor Susuki. They transformed a marshy field into a paradise of shrines, tea houses and plants from the Far East. After decades of decay, there are now proposals for its restoration.

Garden Objects

Gardens would be enhanced by a number of objects including

Trellis work at House of Pitmuies in a garden of lovely old roses and delphiniums.

Trellis work pavilion at Tyninghame sheltering an Italian statue.

From a sketch proposal by Tatham Bailey for a treillage pavilion fronted by statues on pedestals.

Stone term in the herbaceous border at Tyninghame.

pergolas, treillage (or constructions in trellis work), carvings rescued from demolished buildings, statues and sundials.

Treillage was used to define and to screen: and it sometimes joined with murals, mirrors and paths on false perspective, to create *trompe l'oeil* effects. Ornamented treillage fences survive in simple form at Robin's Garden at Kellie Castle, and have been recreated in Lady Haddington's Garden at Tyninghame. There, a 1962 treillage pavilion shelters a marble statue from Vicenza, in a convincing restoration of what once might have been. J. J. Burnet provided splendid pergolas at Fairnalie near Selkirk, as did Paul Waterhouse at Mount Melville. The associated flower gardens may well have been fenced with rustic stems of bent larch, willow, ash or hazel formed into geometric patterns.

The incorporation of genuine antiquities within gardens was partly for conservationist, and partly for enhancement purposes. Lord Somerville re-erected Edinburgh's ancient Mercat Cross in his gardens at the Drum when it was removed from the city centre in 1756 because it impeded traffic. The policies at Fingask are decorated with the Mercat Cross from Perth which had been dismantled by Cromwell's army, whereas that from Cupar was added as a garden decoration to the Hill of Tarvit in 1817. Fragments of the 1639 Parliament House of Scotland decorate the gardens at Arniston, and the remains of much of the fifteenth century Trinity College Church, Edinburgh, removed for the construction of Waverley Station, adorn many Edinburgh gardens including that of Craigcrook Castle.

Statues and Sundials

Garden statuary emphasised the geometric qualities of formal design, and ennobled gateways, vistas and walks. Classical figures were assigned to traditional positions: Pomona was appropriate for an orchard, silent Harpocrates for a grove, ebullient Pan for a glade, Mars or Jupiter for a large lawn, and Neptune for the centre of the largest body of water. Herms (or Terms, or terminal figures, busts standing upon classical plinths which usually taper towards the bottom), were used to denote boundaries.

Statues did not have to be in imitation of classical antiquity. John

64

Macky observed a great avenue leading to an outer court at Glamis in 1729 'which had a statue on each side of the top of the gate as big as the life'.[62] There were further statues against the gateway to the inner court, within which were four brazen statues: James VI in his stole, Charles I in boots, spurs and with a sword as in the Van Dyke painting, Charles II in Roman dress, and James II as painted at Whitehall. The first two, attributed to Arnold Quellin, 1686, survive and have been re-erected on modern plinths.

Early statues were cast in lead, frequently painted. Latterly stone, artificial cast stone, terra cotta and even cast iron were used as appropriate. The high point of lead statue manufacture was the early eighteenth century, and some idea of the range which was achieved may be gauged from the inventory of those within the kitchen garden at Blair in 1757: Bacchus, Flora, Mercury—naturally; but also a piper, fiddler, sailor, harlequin, columbine, a Dutch woman and a Dutchman.

The placing of statues was a matter for some care. If they were not the focal point of axial vistas, they might line riverside walks, such as besides the Venus Isle at Craigiehall, Edinburgh, or along the processional walk at Torosay Castle, Mull. In 1900, nineteen Venetian statues dating from 1698, and carved by Antonio Bonazza in Padua, were installed at Torosay. Believed to be one of the finest collections of seventeenth century statuary outside Italy, they depict huntsmen, gardeners, and fishermen. Nineteenth century rustic figures enliven the topiary at Fingask; carved by David and William Anderson of Perth, they illustrate characters who feature in Burns' poems such as Tam o' Shanter, Kate's Wattie and Meg, and Willie (who brewed a peck o' maut). More unusual sculptured figures greet visitors to Fyvie Castle. One, origin unknown, is a grumpy little dwarf bearing a flintlock, dated 1702 on his breastplate. A sphinx crouches upon his helmet, wings outstretched.

The dark foliage of the topiary at Tyninghame is enhanced by white marble Italianate figures. At Tyninghame can also be found herms, not common in Scotland. There was a preference instead for mythical beasts, particularly griffin and salamander, favourite horses, and pedestal-mounted figures. There is a fine sphinx at Hopetoun House, chained unicorns at Manderston, and slender

Unicorn guarding the steps to the dairy at Manderston.

Planted stone urn at Abbotsford.

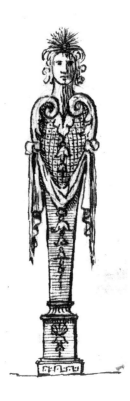

Design for a 'Persian Term', probably by Robert Adam. (Royal Commission on Ancient Monuments, Scotland.)

Statue at Glamis of King Charles by Arnold Quellin, 1686, on a modern plinth.

Statue at Fyvie of an armoured dwarf bearing a flintlock. A sphinx crouches on his helmet.

deer at Gordon Castle. The cast iron silhouettes of deer at Arbuthnott and Inveraray were not for decoration, but for target practice.

Vases and Urns

Points of lesser importance in the policies were marked with vases and urns elevated on one or more plinth or pedestal. The largest vases of the Borghese, Florence or Warwick variety were never intended to be filled with plants: their grandeur alone was considered sufficient. A giant urn thus forms a focal point in the view from Haddo House[63] to the garden beyond, dwarfing twin, flanking, lead stags upon their granite plinths.

Porte-fleurs and *jardinières*, elevated stone structures for plants, were normally confined to flower gardens and conservatories. A number were brought back as souvenirs of trips abroad, particularly

66

Above left
Great stone urn erected 1847
on one of the vistas from
Haddo House.

Above right
Unusual decorated planter on
five fluted columns which was
installed in 1947 at Crathes
but is almost certainly much
older.

Below left
Fountain at Culzean, one of
the most famous properties of
the National Trust for
Scotland.

Below right
Balustrade finial in the form
of an urn with a ram's head at
Mellerstain.

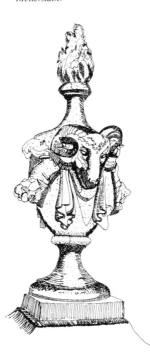

One of twin lead stags on plinths at Haddo, flanking the great urn.

Italianate stone garden seat at Yester.

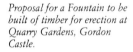

Proposal for a Fountain to be built of timber for erection at Quarry Gardens, Gordon Castle.

from Italy; but by the end of the nineteenth century, most were mass-produced and purchased from catalogues. Of particular interest is a curious planter on fluted columns at Crathes, installed by Lady Burnett of Leys in 1947.

As the garden became an outdoor extension of the house, it was provided with appropriate seats, Italianate stone benches, rustic cast-iron benches or wheelbarrow seats constructed from teak and oak.

Fountains and Wellheads

The fountain symbolised ancient virtues, mysteries, aspirations, and an essential source of water. Sir John Clerk of Penicuik apostrophised his fountain called Scobea: 'more lustrous than glass or even the Horatian fountain of Bandusia itself, surrounded on all sides by trees, and so umbrageous that Diana herself, covered with her nymphs, might use it for a bath'.[64] Rustic wellheads of that type fell into the same category as grottos, in that they were mysterious shrines to be chanced upon in touring the policies.

Fountains closer to the big house, often amid formal gardens, were of a different type. A simple fountain in the gardens at Gordon

Castle consists of a stone basin projected above a pool of water, its plinth heavily inscribed with armorial motifs. A much more elaborate fountain dated 1630 was positioned at Ravelston House, Edinburgh, it takes the form of an obelisk carved with grotesque fish, rising to an armorial finial.

With the nineteenth century revival of formal gardens, there was an equal revival of interest in fountains, foreign sites sometimes being plundered for the benefits of Scots gardens and courtyards. The fountain at Newton, complete with its lion sculptures, was brought back from Italy in 1846. Alternatively, historic Scots examples, such as the fountain at Linlithgow Palace, were used as inspiration; a good copy of which was produced by Charles Doyle, father of Sir Arthur Conan Doyle, in 1859 at Holyrood Palace. Where masonry was unsuitable or too expensive, the client could have recourse to the wide range of cast-iron fountains produced at the foundries; like the one, produced by the Sun Foundry in

Fountain at Ravelston House designed with an array of grotesque creatures, dated 1630.

The King's Fountain at Linlithgow Palace, built circa 1530, was reconstructed 400 years later. (Royal Commission on Ancient Monuments, Scotland.)

One of the sundials at Kelburn.

Sundial from 1675 in the walled garden at Pitmedden.

Baroque sundial at Glamis, circa 1675.

Glasgow, still to be seen at the walled gardens at Traquair near Innerleithen.

Sundials

> What a dead thing is a clock, compared with the simple altar-like structure and heart language of the old dial.

It is sometimes forgotten that in pre-eighteenth century Scotland, clocks were a rarity, and would have to have been set with reference to a sundial. Sundials performed an important practical function, and many were inset into buildings themselves: above the gate at Hatton, into the gazebo at Pitmedden, or even carved in 1686 as a finial over part of the garden wall at Kinross.

The finest Scots sundials, however, are the free-standing, necromantic sundials erected in the seventeenth century. They were sufficiently elaborate and symbolic to form principal wedding presents at dynastic marriages, and, like family furniture, were uplifted and relocated if the owner moved.

The 1562 sundial at Fingask, one of the oldest dials in Europe, takes the form of four rampant lions supporting a capital in the form of a mermaid. That at Holyrood House, carved in 1633 by John

Dialstone at Blair supported by a crouching figure of Time. (Royal Commission on Ancient Monuments, Scotland.)

The sundial at the centre of Drummond Italianate garden.

Sundial at Knipoch Hotel. Around the central gnomon twelve secondary dials indicate the time in places as far afield as Calcutta, Madeira and Peking.

71

Formakin sundial is a centrepiece of the garden laid out from 1900 to a design by Sir Robert Lorimer.

Mylne for £408.15s.6d Scots,[65] is a multi faceted dialstone set upon a baluster carved with heraldic devices including the Royal Arms of Scotland.[66] Upper faces are decorated with 'sinkings' or incised hearts and hemispheres. One gnomon (the upright whose shadow in the sun tells you the time) is formed with the nose of a grotesque face; another is a thistle. The Holyrood dial is a fine example of the family of facet-headed dials which were a particular cultural phenomenon in Scotland in the seventeenth century. They consist of large spherical heads upon a baluster. Relatives of this type include the fine twenty-four-face sundials at Pitmedden, 1675, and nearby Ellon. The 1679 sundial now at Lennoxlove (but originally at North Barr in Lanarkshire), has seventeen faces, and is supported by the sculptured figure of a lady in picturesque contemporary dress, a rose clutched gracefully to her breast. The baroque facet-headed

72

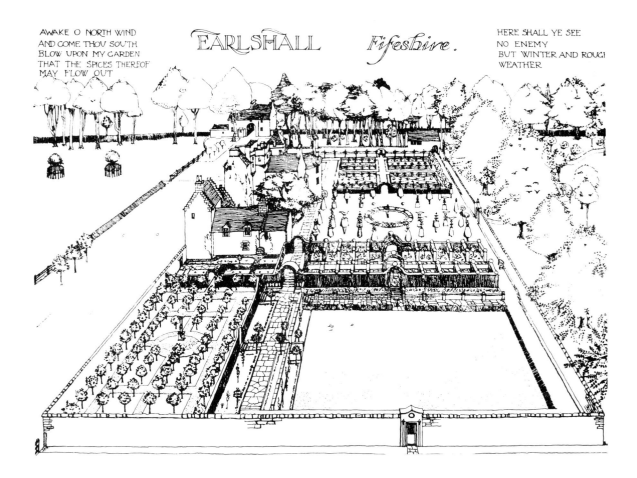

AWAKE O NORTH WIND
AND COME THOU SOUTH
BLOW UPON MY GARDEN
THAT THE SPICES THERFOF
MAY FLOW OUT

EARLSHALL Fifeshire.

HERE SHALL YE SEE
NO ENEMY
BUT WINTER AND ROUGH
WEATHER

sundial at Glamis, erected by the third Earl of Strathmore, some-time between 1671 and 1680, is cut into eighty-four faces, including one for each week of the year; each face with its own gnomon. This sundial is some twenty-one feet high, and is made up of twisted columns and putti, supported by four rampant lions, and crowned with a *fleur-de-lys* over a coronet.

Several of the greatest sundials were carved by the stonemason dynasty of Mylne, from Perth, whose recorded history spans from the fifteenth to the nineteenth centuries, and bred developers, architects, stonemasons, and Master Masons to the Crown of Scotland. Early Mylnes were eminent freemasons of the Lodge of Scone, and it has been questioned whether there might not be a con-

View of Earlshall by H I Triggs dated 1900 emphasises the fundamental importance, to the design, of the enclosing wall around the old tower. Secondary 'walls' of boscage subdivide the garden, many aspects of which survive yet. (Courtesy of the Trustees of the National Library of Scotland.)

nection between the symbols of freemasonry and the sinkings and carvings in those sundials. One of the best known of their products is the 1630 centrepiece to the formal garden at Drummond. Of similar design is the largest sundial at Kelburn, fitted with a weather-vane to its apex. The north and south obelisks added in 1635 to the sundials at Newbattle Abbey, by Dalkeith, are each carried by four curious winged beasts.

The need for skills in dial carving diminished as clocks and portable watches became more common; and so, during the eighteenth century, the more rational 'horological sphere' or 'armillary sundial' increased in popularity. Interconnected metal rings describe a sphere intended to be a representation of the circles of the celestial bodies surrounding the earth. A good example, set upon a sandstone plinth carved with unknown faces, may be seen at Crathes. Although large numbers of sundials were created in the nineteenth century, few were original or significant: most little more than horizontal dials upon a shaft, perhaps carved with an epigram or initials. A sundial outside the Knipoch Hotel, near Oban, has a series of secondary pointers clustered around the gnomon, giving the time in such exotic locations as Buenos Aires and Teheran. The 1810 sundial at Newhall, a memorial to the poet Allan Ramsay, has eight tapering panels inscribed with extracts from the *Gentle Shepherd*.

At the end of the nineteenth century, Sir Robert Lorimer enhanced sundials as he enhanced everything else to do with the formal garden. His square column sundial at Formakin, in gardens now under restoration after fifty years' neglect, has mottos on each face including 'Yesterday Returneth Not' and 'Tomorrow May Never Come'. It stands at the centre of a round pool guarded by four carved lions. Contemporary sundials by Ian Hamilton Finlay, both in his own garden at Little Sparta, and elsewhere, are notable contributions to the art. Little Sparta is virtually a little Wilderness: a wild garden full of secret places with points of deliberate meaning, quirks, inscriptions, sculpture and aphorisms in wood and stone. These are not dedicated to 'bogus philosophers' but depict twentieth century impedimenta including a miniature aircraft carrier containing a birdbath on its runway. There are more than twenty different sundials, with references to classical columns and noble tombs influenced by the landscape paintings of Claude Lorrain.

If one considers how all these buildings may be interrelated in a walled garden, no better example can be seen than that at Earlshall, as remodelled by Sir Robert Lorimer from 1891. It is a particularly good 'room' garden or 'Pleasaunce', subdivided by topiary into a series of miniature gardens of distinctive character. Contemporary drawings indicate an enclosed orchard, set with beehives around a central painted wooden cupid with gilt wings atop a sandstone plinth. There is an apple house with heart shapes cut into the doors; a tool house with carved stone animals on the ridge; and a screen pergola, each one of whose wooden posts was surmounted by a carved and painted wooden parrot. A little summer house, with a patterned wood-block floor, and a carved covered seat with portholes to view the parkland outside, were added later. The gateways are identified with inscriptions like 'Here shall ye see no enemy but winter and rough weather'.

Pavilion in one corner of the walled garden at Earlshall.

75

*The Gladitor Gate at Glamis
is flanked by athletic figures.*

*Substantial timber gates in the
enclosing walls at Wemyss
Castle are linked to coupled
stone gatepiers capped with
two sets of armorial finials in
the form of lions and swans.*

Chapter 3

Enclosure, Cultivation and Improvement

Money to improve and build country estates came from agricultural rents, and the country house was the centre of the Scottish rural economy. Hand-in-hand with the construction of terraces, gardens, landscapes and pretty pavilions, went the reordering of the estate economy, improvements to agriculture; and—not infrequently— the relocation of ancient settlements to new locations out of sight of the big house, on the far side of new enclosing estate walls.

The state of Scots agriculture in the seventeenth century may be gauged by Sir Archibald Grant's description of the estate which his father allowed him to begin to enclose and plant at Monymusk in 1716:

> At that time there was not one acre upon the whole esteat inclosed, nor any timber upon it but a few elm, cycamore, and ash, about a small kitchen garden adjoining the house, and some stragling trees at some of the farmyards, with a small cops wood, not inclosed, and dwarfish and broused by sheep and cattle. All the farmes ill-disposed and mixed, different persons having alternate ridges; not one wheel cariage on the esteat, nor indeed any one road that would alow it, and a rent about £600 sterling per annum; grain and services converted to money. The house was an old castle, with battlements, and six different roofs of various heights and directions, confusedly and inconveniently combined, and all rotten, with two wings more modern, of two storeys only, the half of windowes of the higher riseing above the roofs, with granaries, stables, and houses for all cattle and of the vermine attending them, close adjoining, and with the heath and muire reaching in angles or goushets to the gate, and near much heath near, and what land was in culture belonged to the farmes, by which their cattle and dung were always at the door. The whole land raised and uneven, and full of stones,

many of them very large, of a hard iron quality, and all the ridges crooked in shape of an 'S' and very high, and full of noxious weeds and poor, being worn out by culture, without proper manure or tillage. Much of the land and the muire near the house, poor and boggy; the rivulet that runs before the house in pitts and shallow streams, often varying channel with banks, always ragged and broken. The people poor, ignorant and slothfull, and ingrained enemies to planting, enclosing, or any improvement or cleanness; no keeping of sheep, or cattle, or roads, but four months when oats and bear, (barley) which was the only sort of their grain, was on ground. The farm-houses, and even corne millns, and mans and scool, all poor dirty hutts, pulled in peeces for manure, or fell of themselves almost each alternate year.[67]

He proceeded to enclose, plant and invest in new agricultural methods.

A good example of the consequences of enclosure may be seen at Fochabers, Moray. Of the old village, under the lee of Gordon Castle, survives but one cottage and the Mercat Cross. The model eighteenth century planned town of Fochabers, with its standard gridiron layout straddling the main road from Aberdeen to Inverness, lies some way to the south, on the far side of the estate boundary. The unwashed tenantry removed from view, the policies around the big house would be enclosed by walls: some tall enough and strong enough to deter predators and poachers. All of them were intended to define boundaries and impress visitors. The focus of those enclosing walls was the main gate.

By the later seventeenth century, the symbolic and processional function of gateways required an increasingly impressive response, which was met by carvings, coats-of-arms, and, on occasion, other motifs. When completing his policies at Panmure and at Brechin in 1671, the Earl of Panmure commissioned Alexander Nisbet to construct 'a gate at the chief entry to the court from the west, according to the draught given by Sir William Bruce, and muilds made for that effect'[68] at his house in Panmure, following the completion of the garden dyke. Shortly afterwards, the Earl added gates to Brechin Castle decorated with 'six little flaming urns and decoration foure escalopes and two sinck foills'.[69] A good example of these early gateways is the simple, elegant structure at Hatton House, keystone dated 1692, with fluted pilasters, scroll decorations and a central welcoming acorn. Three new gates were added to Glamis Castle in the late seventeenth century,—the Gladiator Gate, the De'il Gate, and the Church Lodge Gate: all surmounted by grotesque heraldic figures. The best known, the De'il Gate—now the main gate to the park—was originally set up in front of the castle in 1680 by local mason Alexander Crow to a design by Lord Strathmore.

The primitive, tapering obelisks which may be seen on some of the gates of the period—notably at Alloa House, Megginch, and those removed from Castle Huntly, had a bold simplicity which resembled, and may have been connected to, contemporary sundials. We can only guess why so few seventeenth century gates still survive. Presumably improvements in roads, continuing increase in enclosure during the eighteenth century, and the growth in size of carriages may have caused landowners to view old, undersized gateways as archaic, more of an embarrassment than a boast— particularly if they no longer denoted the true extent of one's policies.[70] Of the gates of the earlier period that survived, some were kept for sentimental reasons. Bradwardine bears, emblems of the Maxwell-Stuarts, clasping armorial shields, guard the 1737– 1745 'steekit yetts' at Traquair House near Innerleithen. They have remained firmly closed allegedly since Bonnie Prince Charlie passed through them in 1745, and legend holds that they will be opened again only on the coronation of another Stuart. Railings enriched with ferrous tulips link the gate piers to primitive lodges or shelters at each side of the linden avenue. The gates at Glamis were moved in 1774, and subsequently re-erected when screen walls were added to them in the Tudor Gothic style. The Hatton gateway, moved in 1829, was so carelessly repositioned that its sundial now faces north.

Gateways consist of gates, gate piers, screen walls, and lodges. Visitors following great lengths of an enclosing estate wall, particularly one too high to see over, were expected to come upon the gateway as a foretaste of the mansion within; as the East and West Lodges at Harviestoun, near Dollar were tiny battlemented reflections of the (now demolished) big house. The degree of flamboyance and ostentation was indicative of the pride and conceit of the laird himself: after such a fanfare, the house could sometimes be quite a disappointment. Gates, occasionally wooden, were more usually of cast or wrought iron in patterns ranging from simple spider's webs to elaborate swirling tracery with armorial devices. Customarily, there would be dog bars at the bottom, and at the top an extravagant overthrow (a decorative panel which could be hinged to open to permit the passage of tall carriages). Gates would be hung on piers, usually stone, but occasionally cast-iron, which could be square, oval, circular and sometimes coupled; and whose decoration could include fluting, bands of torus moulding, cushion capitals, cornices, Greek key carving, rustication, and dome caps. Balls, pyramids, mythical beasts and obelisks all serve as finials, although the mid-eighteenth century preferred animals, heraldic beasts or fruit for that purpose. The gate-piers at Largo House, *circa* 1750, are capped by eagles; those at Carmichael House by pineapples; and those at Wemyss Castle by swans and lions. An entry at Arniston is marked by simple iron gates between elaborately carved piers crowned by large stone cats. Known as the 'Cougar Gates' they were made for an Edinburgh property in 1766 and moved to Arniston in 1824.

Gate-piers are joined to the estate perimeter walls by railings, sweeping screen walls, or sometimes a colonnade; save in the very grandest gateways which are swept up into a triumphal arch, whose tympanum would provide a good setting for emblazoning the family crest, mottos or heraldic devices. Triumphal arch gateways, such as James Adam's 1767 Grand Entrance at Cullen House, remained popular right through the early nineteenth century.

The western entrance to Gosford, designed by R. W. Billings in 1854, has screen walls brought up to a tripartite arch, the powerful central opening ornamented with swags and the mottos '*Je Pense*' and '*Forward*'. Asymmetry is provided by the considerable bulk of the West Lodge built into the adjacent screen wall. Another fine gateway is the enthusiastic eruption at Thurso Castle, which is bedecked by thick rope mouldings, fairytale ornament, and cor-belled decoration which rises to, and wraps around, angle bartizans and enriched corbels above a big round-headed entry. The design

Gosford. The West Gate in the form of an exuberant High Victorian triumphal arch in red sandstone, by R W Billings, 1854.

The opulent gateway to Thurso Castle.

has been attributed to Donald Leed, estate architect between 1870 and 1880. The arrangement of an asymmetrically placed lodge, linked to a dramatic stone arch above the entry was a clear success. The Golden Gate at Lanrick, near Doune, probably designed by James Campbell Walker around 1870, embroidered upon the idea by adding an additional pavilion with a conical roof of fish-tailed slates.

The Lodge

The most distinctive feature of most gateways into Scottish estates is the lodge. The earliest type are 'box lodges', consisting of small pavilions by the gate, each box a cube with a flat platform roof. Those at Arniston are topped with a lion on one side, and an elephant the other—the lion for the Dundas family, the elephant for the Oliphants, with whom they intermarried. The boxes scarcely provided generous living accommodation, and seem to have been used principally as daytime shelter for sentries; or occasionally as retirement accommodation for a retainer or gamekeeper. Robert Adam's proposal for an elaborate screened gateway and single lodge at Alva House,[71] 1789, is a little apsed building containing just a kitchen and parlour. Larger lodges were perhaps denied to avoid the twin hazards of children (who might sully the estate entrance), and the possibility of rooms being let for immoral purposes.

Gate-lodges, superior animals to the simple box lodge, became significant from the early nineteenth century and occasionally rose to become a work of considerable architectural importance. They grew and grew in size, eventually to provide quite decent living-space; and the addition of an ogee-shaped roof to the cubic box lodges proved to be a vast visual improvement on their architectural massing.[72] Good examples of the old box lodge in original form can be seen at Castlecraig School, 1791, at Preston Hall, 1795, and at Arniston. The twin 1809 lodges at Megginch are in Gothick style, featuring *quatrefoil* decoration and pointed arches, linked to resited seventeenth century obelisk piers.

Gate-houses and lodges encapsulate changing architectural fashion, and not infrequently claimed a celebrated architect as their designer. The fine 1820 South Lodge at Keir, Bridge of Allan, is a

Preston Hall box lodges and screen walls by Robert Mitchell, 1795. The Coade-stone lions stand above cast-iron gates with spiderweb patterning.

Kinross. One of twin gatelodges built in 1905, but clearly looking back to an earlier era. The original box lodges were demolished in 1810.

magnificent neo-classical design by David Hamilton (1768–1843), one of Scotland's finest architects. A central, projecting drum contains a living room; and the three other rooms—two with bed recesses, and the pantry—give an indication of the increasing size of such buildings.[73] William Robertson's 1838 East Lodge at Aberlour House is a Doric temple of some elegance, while its counterpart West Lodge by Robertson's nephews A. & W. Reid, is Italianate with overhanging eaves and a campanile. Archibald Simpson designed an octagonal, two-storeyed lodge in Greek Revival style for Gordon Castle at Fochabers, given simple dignity by its wide-bracketed eaves and low-pitched roof. Four turrets with conical roofs and grotesque finials flank the splendid 1819 castellated gate-house at Fyvie, whereas the central arched gateway of the South Lodge at Duns, dating from the following year, is sandwiched between a round tower on one side, and a square turret on the other.

Beyond the confines of Gothick or Classical, a goodly number of more bizarre gates and lodges were constructed.[74] Taymouth, which had several, offers a castellated lodge loosely based on medieval imagery, a rustic lodge formed of knobbly larch posts set with deer heads, and essays in crude craggy stonework at Rock and Delarb Lodges. Other idiosyncratic gateways include twin ivy-clad Magical Arches at Spottiswoode House, each decorated with five little obelisks; and the curiosity of the massive masonry piers at Netherurd House, which support no more than a whalebone overthrow. Ury House is guarded by ink-bottle lodges, with central chimneys that peep through the steep conical roofs.

The beautiful lodge at Ballindalloch Castle, Aberlour, by Thomas MacKenzie is an early example of Scottish Baronial, modified with grace and elegance. It carries the delightful MacPherson motto 'Touch not the cat bot (without) a glove'. Considerably grander, and a magnificent sight for miles, are the tall French Chateaux that Marshall MacKenzie (Thomas's son) designed as a gigantic east gateway to Dunecht House near Aberdeen. Erected in 1923, the gates are inscribed with the motto 'Do it With Thy Might'.

Romantics preferred gateways in the form of fortified bridges, examples of which can be seen at Culzean, Milton Lockhart, and

The East Lodge at Aberlour, distinguished by an Italianate campanile, dates from 1856. (Photo by Charles McKean.)

Greek-Revival East Lodge at Gordon Castle showing features characteristic of that style – such as the low-pitched roof with wide-bracketed eaves soffit. (Royal Commission on Ancient Monuments, Scotland.)

*Symmetrical gatelodge at
Fyvie Castle leading into
parkland which was
landscaped in the early
eighteenth century.*

The Glen. John Paterson's design for the gate-lodge at Monzie, near
Comrie, is itself a miniature castle, and to arrive there by horse-
drawn carriage in the half light must have been an exhilarating
experience: just past a little outer lodge, the battlemented tower of
the main gate lodge would come into view, soon seen to be part of
a composition of pepperpot turrets, arrow-slit windows and crenellations. A more striking version of the same can be found at
Blackcraig, in the remote district of Strathardle. An unprepossess-
ing lodge facing the road shelters behind a pair of fine, garlanded
gate-piers carved with Gothick motifs, and guarded by two obser-
vant stone dogs. Pass this and go down hill. An edifice in a class all
of its own comes into view, above a wide-span bridge arching over
the River Ardle. It is a strange confection of finials, battlements and
bridges in the air, mostly executed in a hard stone which has leached
white stalactites from its joints. It represents an old man's fancy.
The eccentric artist Patrick Allan Fraser was over sixty, and wished
to embellish a pre-existing bridge by building above it. He enjoyed
the 'game' of building, and enjoined quirky contractual details. The
stone, for example, had to be gathered from the fields. That the big
house itself is anything other than an acute disappointment is
remarkable. Patrick Allan Fraser had been responsible for restoring
the ancient house of Hospitalfield (Sir Walter Scott's *Monkbarns*)
near Arbroath.

Most estates of size would have at least two lodges: the main one
guarding the principal drive to the house, the other the subsidiary
drive past the stables or steading. Larger estates could garner entire
collections of lodges: both Dalmeny and Taymouth had at least
eight. Nor was there any need for them to be consistent in style.
Theorists of the picturesque believed that the lodge should be
designed in sympathy with its own location, rather than in style with
the big house. A number of small lodges detached from gateways
were proposed on the estate at Inveraray: a lochside structure with
battlements, spire and dome for the Duke's fishermen; and, at each
end of the Garron Bridge, lodges linked with abutments to arched
screen walls. Two lodges designed by Alexander Nasmyth, in
1802–3 survive: the 'Hexagon' is a little Gothick waterfall-viewing
pavilion near Carloonan. The 'beehive cottage' up in the woods, was

*One of two rubble built
arches at Spottiswoode each
crested with five obelisks.*

At Dunecht the mighty lodges form an entrance visible for miles around Loch of Skene.

Taymouth medieval-inspired lodge displaying genuine armorial panels.

probably built for the supervisor of the nearby limekiln. Completely round with a conical roof, there is only one room within, a segment reserved as a kitchen, all focused upon a central chimney stack.

The growth of sporting estates, and an increasing reliance on pattern book designs, eroded the impulse for eccentric gate-lodges with unique architectural qualities. In the remoter parts of Scotland, where a local architect might not be cheaply available, designs from pattern books offered a convenient alternative. The nobility of the gate-lodges was further damaged by its incorporation as a marker for Victorian civic institutions in towns, such as zoos, cemeteries, public parks and hospitals. By the end of the nineteenth century, it had become something of a debased item, and its dignity was only retrieved by the designs of Sir Robert Lorimer and his followers. The gate at Balmanno, Bridge of Earn, forms a visual frame which 'intensifies the effect of the house'[75]: in other words, recreates a

sense of enclosure. The gate-house at Balcarres, 1898, has heraldic beasts on the gate-piers to complement the silhouette of a grotesque figure blowing a horn on top of its pyramid roof. Ferrous tulips can be found in the iron overthrow at Pitkerro (1903) while at Briglands, a grotesque bird's nest in stone is to be seen on the ridge. The most striking of Lorimer's lodge designs can be found at Formakin, near Bishopton. Stone monkeys can be seen chasing each other along the ridges of all of the buildings in the complex. Formakin is a magnificent, unfinished essay in seventeenth century Scots architecture, and it is thought that the inspiration for the lodge may have been Queen Mary's Bath House in Edinburgh. Yet the essentially functional nature of these structures is embodied in the fact that the Formakin gate-house was fitted with machinery so that the gates could open automatically.

One of two 'ink-bottle' lodges at Ury House.

At Blackcraig this splendid
eccentric structure combines a
lodge above a bridge.

Formakin gatelodge is built of
a lovely honey-coloured
rubble with stone dressings
around windows and an
armorial panel above the
worm-and-cog operated main
gates. (Royal Commission on
Ancient Monuments,
Scotland.)

Craigmin Bridge built circa 1780 is an inspired example of whimsy which is also practical. (Royal Commission on Ancient Monuments, Scotland.)

The cast iron bridge at Stracathro by William Atkinson, 1828.

Proposal by Robert Adam for a gothick bridge – perhaps an exercise in style rather than a genuine intention to build. (Royal Commission on Ancient Monuments, Scotland.)

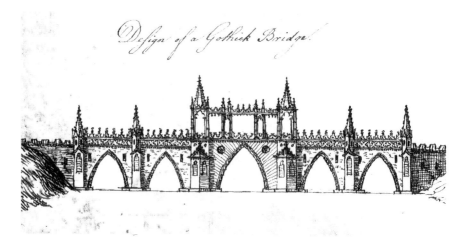

Design of a Gothick Bridge

Bridges

Bridges were raised above their utilitarian function to become the object of views, and the source from which views could be achieved. Underlying their construction was the belief that in a bridge lay a supreme example of man's control over nature. Such was its importance that an artificial lake was created at Pitfour solely for the opportunity of bridging it in a fine manner. Many older houses and castles, built in semi-fortified positions on the edge of ravines or on a peninsula surrounded on three sides by water, required new bridges once security ceased to be important. Not infrequently, that was done in a sumptous manner. William Adam's bridge streaks out from Cullen House towards the Bin Hill, over the Punch Bowl; and his son Robert's dramatic Montagu Bridge does likewise over the River Esk by Dalkeith Palace. In addition to the main span, the latter provides subsidiary arches for the new picturesque paths along the riverbanks. Relocation of ancient communities distant from the house led to a comparable resiting of the principal roads that used to run through them. That was the genesis of the two splendid bridges at Inveraray, by Roger Morris and Robert Mylne.

Bridges carrying the principal drive to the house had picturesque duties, and the style was selected according to function, location and client. There were graceful Classical bridges, bristly Gothick bridges, truly rustic bridges, Chinese bridges, Tudor bridges, and iron bridges. In the case of Kildrummy, the garden was graced with

The stables at Kinross present a magnificent facade of polished grey ashlar to the main drive. The frontage is extended back to form a quadrangle dominated by a doocot.

a magnificent replica of the Old Brig o' Balgownie.[76] Cast iron was used at Stracathro to form a three-arched neo-Tudor bridge with mullioned spandrels, to an 1828 design by William Atkinson. Many bridges invite curiosity by their apparent eccentricity. That at Raehills has three arms, two on the east bank of Kinnel Water, and one on the west leading to the house. At the intersection of the arms, a masonry column provides support for the footways which meet in a pavilion with a conical thatched roof.

The Court of Offices

The Court of Offices was a descendant of the buildings contained within the barmkin wall of the tower house, and contained buildings necessary for the efficient functioning of the occupants of the house. They formed the service centre, and once they became larger, more efficient, and possibly more offensive, they became separated from the house. One of the earliest surviving examples of a complete court separate from the house was built at Kinross in 1690, to designs by Sir William Bruce. Its symmetrical façade of coursed rubble is flanked by ogee-roofed pavilions, and fronts a quadrangular courtyard with a central doocot. It is important to distinguish

The 'round square' at Gordonstoun has been converted into schoolrooms and a library yet retains its original function of a shelter. (Royal Commission on Ancient Monuments, Scotland.)

these buildings from farms and farm steadings. These, the 'laigh biggings', would contain the rooms that drove the household: the brewhouse, the bakehouse, stores, slaughterhouse, milk-house, coal and ash houses, the dairy and the riding stables: or a variety of those. In the late seventeenth century, there grew a deviant version, the curiously titled 'round squares': round courts of offices of which singular examples remain at Dallas, just south of Elgin, and at nearby Gordonstoun. Now part of Gordonstoun school, the latter is a splendid rubble-built circle of largely two-storey crow-stepped buildings. Its form was thought, by locals, to have been devised by the Wizard of Gordonstoun, Sir Robert Gordon, to meet necromantic requirements. A shade too fanciful: the arrangement gives excellent protection from the wind, and that was why it was copied, in 1796, by Robert Mylne, who adapted the round square form for a steading in Gothick style, at Maam, Inveraray. Maam was equipped with special walls and a battened floor to dry corn and hay right up to Christmas; and a flagged floor for drying potatoes and facilities for threshing. Dorothy Wordsworth was not impressed seeing only: 'broad, outspreading, fantastic and unintelligible buildings'.[77] A similarly half-completed, late eighteenth century

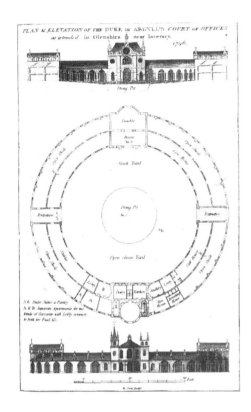

round square, now converted into a visitors' centre at Aden, has a powerful tower inset with Venetian and Diocletian windows. Its pyramid roof, which shelters a doocot, is capped by a little rotunda. Other complete examples of 'round squares' can be found at Prestonfield House Hotel, Edinburgh, designed in 1816 by James Gillespie Graham and now a conference centre, and the fantastic, circular stables at Errol Park, 1811, whose pedimented entry has a three-storey belvedere tower above, which changes in character from a square to an octagon.

Although Gothick seems to have been a popular mid-eighteenth century style for courts of offices, exemplified by the fine structure at Largo House, 1750, with its crenellations and *quatrefoils* of a mock military sort, mainstream Classical was more common. John Adam's design for stables called Cherry Park at Inveraray formed a classical quadrangle, with cube pavilions decorated with Venetian windows in each corner. Contemporary offices of bakehouse,

Maam farm, Inveraray, from a 1798 engraving for 'A General View of Agriculture in the County of Argyll' by James Robson. (RCAHMS)

Belvedere tower at Errol stables, commenced 1811, with later additions.

brewhouse and stables at Penicuik were considerably more theatrical: a spire after the fashion of James Gibbs soars above the main entrance pend. A local story has it that the spire was originally designed for the local kirk, but was rejected by the elders as inappropriate. It is a testimony to the importance of those courts that when Penicuik House was burnt down in 1899, the Clerk family found the suitably converted court more than adequate a substitution. Much the same transformation is currently happening at Tyninghame.

A watershed in agricultural improvement was the passing of the Montgomery Act in 1770.[78] It enabled landlords, particularly proprietors of entailed estates, to debit three-quarters of the cost of new offices to their heirs; and it was followed by a period of enthusiastic building. The eleventh Earl of Eglinton rebuilt all his steadings near Irvine in the 1770s. In the last quarter of the eighteenth century, some 500 new steadings were constructed in Berwickshire; and between 1770 and 1810, ninety-nine per cent of all farmhouses in Ayrshire were rebuilt.[79] The confidence created by the new Act is reflected in the following letter from the farm manager at Culzean in 1775: 'I have not a proper farmyard, nor a house or shed for feeding cattle, or for the convenience of raising as much dung as might be made; but these things will come in course. Lord Cassillis has an extensive and very commodius plan of offices which he intends to build very soon'.[80] The offices, finally built by Robert Adam in 1780, were indeed extensive and commodious, in a castellated style, with Fort George pepperpots above the ceremonial entrances. It is now converted into the Visitors' Centre which hosts exhibitions. Following Culzean, Adam designed additions to a traditional block at Gosford, near Aberlady, making it classical with inset relief panels in Coade stone. Its parapet is surmounted by urns and sphinxes, with a 1792 clock by Veitch of Haddington set into the tympanum. Adam's proposals for Dalquharran, Fullarton, and Kirkdale House were much larger. An irregular 'D' shaped court of offices was planned for Kirkdale,[81] dominated by the enormous drum of a stable block, containing eighteen stalls radiating from the centre. His unrealised scheme for offices at Alva House comprised an immense circle of buildings enclosing a spired, central doocot.

The Pleasance or walled garden at Edzell shelters geometric planting with high decorated walls.

Cougars crouch on imposing
cylindrical gatepiers decorated
with rustication and carved
swags at Arniston.

Twin lodges of deep red
sandstone and massive
gatepiers joined with a crested
iron arch are a fitting end to a
long tree lined approach
avenue at Yester.

Blind windows conceal a
doocot below the spire that
dominates the courtyard at
Rosebery.

Twin pavilions in the walled
garden at Preston Hall; they
rise from a cross-wall which
subdivides the garden.

Drummond Castle Italianate garden viewed from the terrace above.

Garden pavilion built into the enclosing walls around Dirleton Castle.

View from Dunrobin Castle down to parterres which stretch almost to the seashore.

Even unglazed, and with its parterre long overgrown, the conservatory at Dalkeith Palace remains an imposing structure.

The remote Bullough mausoleum on the National Nature Reserve island of Rhum.

The cottage ornée at Mellerstain, with its own fenced-in knot garden, possibly converted from a redundant doocot.

A banquetting house and dog kennel were combined at Chatelherault, its baroque facade fronting a formal garden.

The gateway into the walled garden at Preston Hall was modified in 1888.

*William Adam's West Bridge,
erected in 1744, takes
advantage of the dramatic
setting of Cullen House.*

Accommodation was planned for fowls, pigs, calves, cows, rooms for the carpenter, poultrymaid, dairymaid, a laundry, bakehouse, washhouse, scullery, brewhouse and boiling room; a parlour and offices for the steward; a slaughterhouse, coach-house, smith's shop, stables, tack room and cart-shed.[82] Such Promethean schemes seem to have died with the outbreak of war with France in 1793.

As with almost everything else on the improved estate, courts of offices and steadings had a decorative function. Generally of square or rectangular plan, many were set to one side, but within view of the house; the secondary drive leading past it. In consequence, the façade facing the house had a grandeur denied to the rest of the complex, and in earlier years usually comprised a symmetrical palace frontage, flanked by corner pavilions, focused upon a central entrance beneath the pend. The entrance was frequently pedimented

Penicuik stables. Archive drawings indicate stables, coachhouses, brewhouse, henhouse, doghouse, cowhouse, infirmary, hogs sty, slaughterhouse, barn, smiths and wrights shop, workmans hall and a central midden. It is now a private house.

Proposals at Kirkdale House by Robert Adam for a great circular stables (with radiating stalls) fronting a 'U' plan court of offices. (Courtesy of Sir John Soane's Museum.)

Robert Adam designed frontage to stables as Gosford, contrasting grey stone dressings with orange-brown dressed rubble. Swans, urns and a sphinx add to the decoration.

or graced with a bell or clock tower. A soaring lead spire above an octagonal clock tower acts as the centrepiece at Blackadder Mount. The entrance to that at Rosebery House is beneath a dramatic, vertically proportioned Gothick façade capped by a spire. At Lanrick the entrance arch is topped with a swept-roofed square tower with little bartizan turrets, through which strange anthropomorphic apertures give access to the doocot within. An excellent cupola at Saltoun Mains caps a leaded dome atop an octagonal ashlar drum containing, yet again, a doocot.[83] Another above the stables at Tillicoultry takes the form of a fine baroque design with a clock on each face. A cupola caps the pedimented central pavilion of the 1763 design for a court of offices by Sir William Chambers at Duddingston; here kitchens and servants' quarters to the south, are linked by a Doric colonnade to the pedimented stable wing to the north. One of the finest steadings in the picturesque manner is Alexander Nasmyth's essay *circa* 1800 at Roseneath Castle.

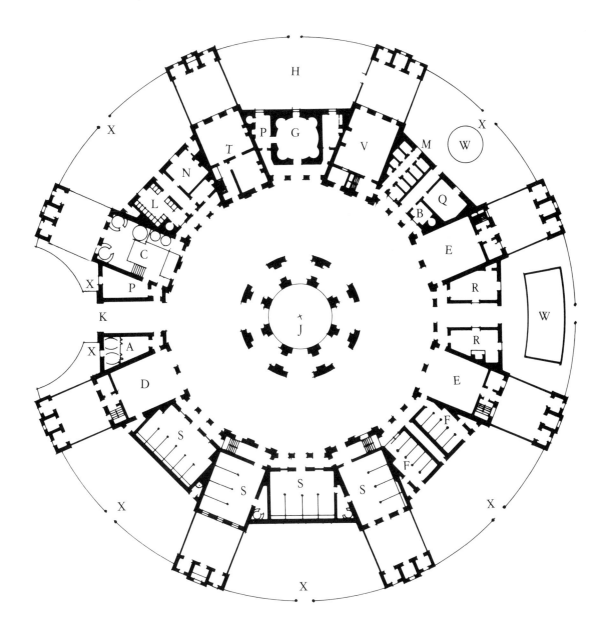

Alva House. Unrealised proposals on an epic scale by the Adam Brothers for offices 'in the Castle Style' for John Johnstone.
For notation, see end of Selective Gazetteer.

But the sheer requirements of space, in addition to a growing dislike for the messy side of agriculture, led to a complete separation of stables from the court of offices. The Victorians tended to integrate the offices back into wings extending behind the house,

whereas stables and kennel courtyards became distinctive buildings in their own right.[84] Well into the eighteenth century, farmers had been reluctant to replace oxen by horses for work on the farm, as oxen were more reliable, cheaper, stronger, and less prone to disease, damage and excitable fright. It is probable that the move from oxen to the horse was hastened by the invention of the swing plough in 1760, since it required only a team of two horses as compared to the ten or twelve oxen needed for the heavy Scots plough. Once the value of the work horse was fully appreciated, it became indispensable to the economy of the rural estate until the arrival of the tractor.

The stable block shared similar visual characteristics as steadings and courts of offices. The eighteenth century block at Whim House foreshadowed what became the norm. It was entered through a portico, flanked by ornamental niches, the wings on either side containing stalls divided by carved, monolithic stone slabs. Each stall was served by a stone feeding trough filled by a chute from the hay loft upstairs (although first floor hay lofts became generally unpopular since it was feared that dust from upstairs could cause respiratory troubles for horses below). Pavilions at each end con-

At Blackadder the spire completes a clocktower which sits uneasily above the pend.

Rosebery Mains is dominated by a spire.

tained coach-houses, tack rooms, and stone staircases rising to groom's quarters above.

Many stable blocks derived therefrom, with the vocabulary of a central entrance identified by pediment, dome, lantern or tower, then wings to either side, sometimes arcaded and frequently bizarre, containing loose boxes. At either end, sometimes pedimented, pavilions contained coach-houses, tack rooms and accommodation above. All these elements combined to form the horse palace at Cambuswallace, designed in 1809 by William Stirling. Its entrance, signalled by a lead spire upon a high octagonal stone tower, has wings on either side containing stalls, and end pavilions serving as coach-houses. Where the site was too cramped for a full courtyard, accommodation would be squeezed into a taller block, exemplified by Stirling's heavy, symmetrical design at Alva House, halfway up the Ochils. There is ground floor accommodation for seventeen horses, flanked by a coach-house pavilion at each end. Rooms for coachmen, butler, gamekeeper and groom are above. The focus of the design is the Venetian window below a pyramid roof at the centre. The feature above the entrance to stables at The Haining

101

At Duddingstone a baroque
clocktower crowns the centre
of the offices; wings each side
are reached by arcades.

The 'H' plan range at
Lanrick, sadly derelict, is
dominated by a square tower
housing a doocot.

is of a different sort: the skull of a horse which killed the Laird.

Elaborate stables built for thoroughbreds and racehorses became more common in the late nineteenth century, and are exemplified by that at Manderston. The client is said to have instructed the architect John Kinross that no expense be spared: and the result is delightful. A central cobbled courtyard is entered through an arch, decorated with wall carvings of a hunt in full cry. Within may be found a tack room, finished with mahogany fittings and a marble floor. Stalls and loose boxes are designed with brass posts and fittings, under a vaulted ceiling of polished teak. Horses' names, all beginning with 'M' like Mango and Malakoff, are carved on marble panels above each feeding trough.

The Steading

From *circa* 1790, there was considerable rebuilding of farm steadings architecturally similar to stables. Initially quadrangular or rectangular, different plan forms—such as 'H' plan, 'U' plan or 'E' plan came to become adopted latterly, as farming became more technical. These buildings represented the heart of the agricultural estate, and considerable care and attention was lavished upon their planning. A medium-sized steading would probably comprise a cartshed, straw barn, corn barn, boiler house, cow byre, feeding byre, turnip house, base for calves, piggery, court for young cattle, stable, loose box, and provision for hay. The upper storeys, if any, would include a granary, more straw barns, and a loft for sheep. Attention was paid to a logical sequence of uses, and the careful provision both of power, and of collection points for manure. Sometimes, power was provided by a horse engine-house against the outer perimeter, usually against the corn barn.

Architectural pretension was generally reserved for the façade visible from the house and drive, and sometimes rose to considerable grandeur. The early example at Hill of Tarvit by Cupar, has a symmetrical palace-front, the end pavilions of which display superb, giant glass fanlights. By *circa* 1840, the fashion for good, plain, classically symmetrical steadings began to crumble before a wave of romanticism and, sometimes, medievalism. At Hospitalfield, near Arbroath, Patrick Allan Fraser remodelled his home farm by the addition of deliberately incomplete pieces of building such as a spurious '16th century gatehouse'. His intention was to create a composition which gave the appearance of being a ruinous castle, half rebuilt as a steading. In the 1850s, several treatises on the design of farm buildings were published—such as *Rural Architecture* by the Coldingham architect William Gray, and the *Architecture of the Farm* by John Starforth. The planning of the building taking precedence over the architecture, the style was plain and functional, and chimneys began to appear attached to boiler houses.

The steading at Keir is possibly the closest Scotland reached to an ornamental farm, and is founded upon an 1832 decorated farm stead designed by David Bryce. Rubble walls are given form by dressed quoins, dentil courses, and an elaborate variety of dressed stone panels and carvings, which include the heads of farm animals. The clock tower is banded with red and white glazed tiles, and features a number of aphorisms such as 'Our time is a Very Shadow that Passeth Away', or 'Tis Later with the Wise than He's Aware'. Even more eccentric, in splendid seventeenth century style, is the court at Formakin by Sir Robert Lorimer, now converted to a museum and tearoom. Above the entrance arch is the date stone '1694 DL'. D L stands for 'damned lie!': it was built in 1911.

Chapter 4

Decorative Larders

Before the agricultural improvements of the eighteenth century, the common diet in rural Scotland consisted of milk products, fish, and produce from the rigs and kailyard, seasonally supplemented, where sanctioned by the laird, by fish from 'stanks' (fishponds), rabbits from 'cunningaries', and birds from doocots. Fresh meat was occasionally available, but in limited quantities; and until root vegetables were grown on a sufficiently large scale for winter feed, such rare meat as there was, remained seasonal, as observed in the 1770s: 'There is hardly any such thing as mutton to be had till August, or beef till September; that is to say, in quantity fit to be eaten; and both go out about Christmas. Therefore at or about Martinmass, such of the inhabitants who are anything beforehand with the world, salt up a quantity of beef, as though they were going on a voyage'.[85] Daniel Defoe judged the pickled pork packed in Aberdeen as 'the best cured for keeping on long voyages of any in Europe'.[86]

Buildings were needed to grow, breed and store that supply of flesh, fish, and fowl. From the late seventeenth century, they acquired architectural qualities which transformed them from utilitarian structures to pavilions of consequence. Thus the doocot, the icehouse, the game-larder and the dairy rose from their functional origin.

Icehouses

> The Icehouse forms an excellent larder for the preservation of every kind of food liable to be injured by heat in summer: . . . and for the table, where coolness is desirable, the use of ice in summer is a great luxury.
>
> J. B. Papworth 1818
> *Rural Residences*

Sometimes, again, we would only walk . . . as far as the icehouse,
a strange, forbidding cave, seemingly ancient as the beehive
tombs of Mycenae, to peer down its shaft full of a century's
drifting of leaves, a place still set apart for winter even in the
midst of summer.

Osbert Sitwell 1945
Left Hand, Right Hand

The Icehouse

The icehouse was an important feature of domestic economy. It was
a primitive refrigerator, usually a man-made cavern (although caves
and grottos were also used), part filled with ice. It stored meat carcasses, fish in barrels, beer and wine for chilling, confectionery and
spring water. Bottles were generally wrapped in chaff and set into
the ice itself, whereas other produce was placed in matting on top.
Fruit, vegetables and dairy products were more likely to be
suspended on wooden trays in the cool air above, or placed on stone
shelves in the passage or the gallery.

At first, the ice was most likely to be collected from estate ponds
and lochs by means of punts and ice-poles, and thus occasionally
contained leaves and mud – to the disgust of some commentators.
It seems it was not until large quantities of purer ice from America
and Scandinavia became available in the nineteenth century that ice
was used in food itself to any extent; moulded with fruit into cold
edible goblets, shaped into edible coats of arms, used to form
ornamental ice turrets, decorated with flowers which could be set
on the sideboard to cool hot rooms in summertime. It was
undeniably popular. The *Ice Book* published by Thomas Masters in
1844, contained recipes including coffee ice-cream and nesselrode,
or frozen pudding.[87] Ice was also used medicinally. In a letter of
1824, Sir Walter Scott described how the life of one of his friends
had been saved by the application of ice to cool a fever brought on
by a hunting accident. He noted that there had been only one day
in the previous winter when it had been possible to collect ice to
stock the icehouse, and implied that this was not an unusual
application.

Most icehouses were free-standing structures, positioned as close

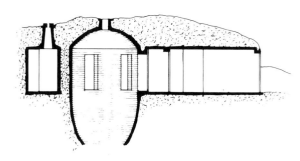

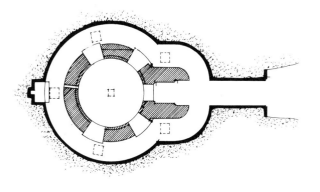

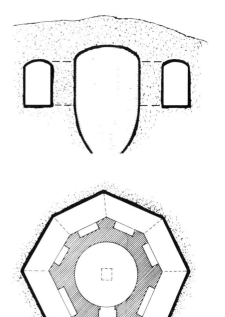

Survey drawings (1984) of galleried icehouses at Alva (left) and Mortonhall (right) The latter seems to have been modified circa 1940 for use as an air-raid shelter. Openings were cut in the chamber linking the gallery to a false floor.

At Gosford, the door into the icehouse is hidden within this rustic frontage of tufa, pebbles, shells and glass which is capped with an encrusted cross, fronting an ornamental lake.

107

as possible to the kitchen court while still allowing for an easy delivery of ice. A sloping riverside, or, as at Culzean, a lakeside site, was ideal to allow drainage from the base of the ice-chamber. Damp was thought to be the main enemy of ice, and William Cobbett recommended that icehouses be sited away from the shade of trees, and that the entry door should face south-east. A stepped platform by an entry door, set beneath an ashlar pediment at the side of a grassy, egg-shaped hump, was its upmarket appearance; the entry to many was almost invisible – that to Penicuik House no more than an opening along the wall of the ha-ha. The picturesque approach to the icehouse at Arbuthnott leads down a fine winding stone stair-case set into a steep riverbank, whereas that to Broxmouth icehouse is related axially to a sundial court overlooking an ornamental lake. The icehouse at Gosford is disguised behind the rusticated façade of a picturesque grotto made of tufa, glass and pebbles, within which are stone seats. High ornamental schemes proposed by Sir John Soane and John Papworth in England for the incorporation of icehouses within neo-classical pavilions were little emulated in Scotland; although the ornamental ogee-roofed pavilion beside the drive at Murdostoun (1790) combined an icehouse with a doocot.

In most icehouses, the entry door led to a flagged passage running straight and level for between one and three metres, subdivided by a number of insulating doors ideally edged with leather to give a draught-proof seal.[88] Typically, the icehouses at Dalkeith was an aggrandised version, with four doors, and a passageway with three bends. Charles McIntosh recommended that the voids between the doors be back-filled with straw to improve insulation, (although it would hardly have aided access). Access to the icehouses at Alva House and Morton Hall is along a passage which broadens into a shelved gallery running around the outside of the chamber itself.

The icehouse chamber can be a fine dramatic space, and tends to be one of three forms: cubed, egg-shaped, or bottle-shaped. The most simple type was a rubble-built cube-shaped void, with a barrel vaulted roof like that at Colzium and Charleston. More dramatic, however, is the pure egg-shaped void sculpted out of fine ashlar stonework (Whim), or brick (Broxmouth). The internal diameter varied from between two and a half to five metres, and the height

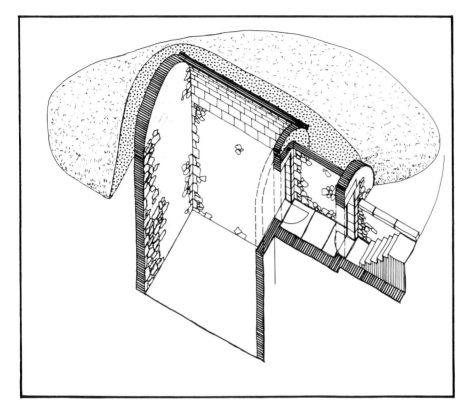

Cut-away view of a typical barrel vaulted icehouse. For best results, a drain at the base of the chamber would lead meltwater via a trap into a stream.

from four to seven metres. Generally, the passageway entered the chamber several metres above its base.

Ideally, meltwater at the base of the chamber discharged through a drain down to the bed of a nearby stream or loch; protected by a trap to keep out warm air, rodents and insects. A sump above the drain outlet would be protected by a cartwheel, cast-iron grating, or even, on occasion, a perforated stone. The absence of a drain could be expected to have a bad effect on the performance of the icehouse; and indeed poor drainage may have been the reason for the failure to form a satisfactory icehouse in the vaults at Inveraray Castle in the early 1780s. Expert help failed to solve the problem: 'It did not answer'[89]; and in 1786, a free-standing icehouse built by William Stothard of Arrochar was completed by the stable block in less than four months. It cost just over £25 including ice and Stothard's fee: good value, considering that the James Adam-designed icehouse at Cullen had cost £5 more some ten years earlier.

Virtually all icehouse chambers were covered with earth, partly to help resist the thrust of the vault, but more importantly to increase thermal insulation which was also achieved by using thatched roofs on timber frames.

A skilled well-digger was considered a suitable man to construct an icehouse, and the specification for that at Luffness, dating from 1847, indicates the high quality of construction that was required:

> Walls to be cross band laid best stone. External walls and roof puddled with clay to one foot thickness. Whole interior to be in well squared rubble carefully bedded . . . Roof arches with stone dressed to the radius and the porch laid with droved pavement. Drain built with clean hammer-dressed stone and the cesspool will be made of cast iron . . . Interior door of two thicknesses of one and a quarter inch deal nailed across each other grooved tongued and beaded on edges, hung with crook and bank hinges and provided with a strong malleable iron bolt . . . Exterior door framed with two and a quarter inch wood in four panels . . . hung with eight inch hinges and provided with an eight inch rimmed lock.[90]

Workmen filled the icehouse by first placing an insulating layer of straw over the sump and around the inside of the chamber. The ice was then compacted in layers with straw or sawdust. Some icehouses, like that at Arbuthnott, were top-loaded, the ice shot down through a hole in the crown of the vault. It was an easier procedure than carrying it along entry passages with changes in direction, and the *Book of the Garden* illustrates a canvas conveyor-belt system to assist such top-loading. When the ice became level with the entry passage, the surface would be dished to fall inwards. The workmen would then cover it with rushes, straw or even old sailcloth, and then retire to get warm again. A freezing mixture of saltpetre (potassium nitrate) sometimes mixed with salt, ammonia and muriates of soda would aid consolidation and congelation of the main body of the refrigerating ice,[91] if it were not to be used for culinary purposes.

Inconvenience and the invention of the portable icebox led to the demise of the free-standing icehouse. It was first moved closer to the kitchen offices: as witness the enormous six metre high brick chamber, in flattened pear shape, at Stobo Castle which is built among the domestic offices between brewhouse, laundry, slaughterhouse and tack rooms; and at Manderston, a tiny top-loaded ice-chamber adjacent to the basement kitchens in the main house which must have been replenished with ice from a larger reservoir. But even the new proximity of the ice chamber to the house did not save it. The refrigerator became altogether more convenient.

Icehouses are splendid structures, but not easy to adapt. Many have been filled in with earth, rubbish or worn-out family furniture. Others have been sealed up and forgotten (and they are difficult to find). There are restored examples at Duff House, Culzean and Rossdhu, but they have iron safety grills installed to prevent children or animals falling into the chamber and being unable to get out again. It is sad that access to these remarkable structures, which require little enough maintenance, should be so restricted. The echoing, eerie atmosphere within can be remarkable.

The Dairy

Visiting Iona in 1760, Bishop Pocock was 'conducted to a house where Eggs, Cheese, Butter and Barley Cake were served, and a large bowl of Curds'.[92] It was probably a dairy; and indicates the social, if not ceremonial role that some dairies were expected to fulfil. The estate dairy was the building that perhaps went further than any other in combining necessary practicality with pursuit of pleasure, whether free-standing or incorporated into the kitchen court. One of the earliest surviving examples of free-standing dairies is a harled cube with a pyramid roof at Dipple, near Fochabers. It still contains original cheese-making equipment. From such plain beginnings, dairies developed into ornamental structures, and an important stop for a cool and refreshing break during the estate tour.

The preferred temperature within was ten degrees centigrade; for cream would sour quickly in hotter conditions, and would fail to coagulate at lower temperatures. This need for coolness had inevitable consequences for the design. Trees were used for shade

111

Manderston dairy is finished internally with several colours of marble and a vaulted ceiling terminating in a carved boss depicting a serene cow and milkmaid.

Archive view inside the dairy at Millearne. (Royal Commission on Ancient Monuments, Scotland.)

(although it was important to avoid vegetation becoming so close that it could taint the milk), and dairies were often located in a paddock with a pheasantry or apiary. Some used thatched roofs as architectural imagery and for practical reasons, both for insulation and to allow a controllable circulation of air within (as at Glamis). Slatted verandahs were occasionally used as *brises-soleil*, and stained glass was used to cut out the brightest sunshine at Balboughty Dairy. Finishes within were ceramic, cool and easily cleaned: marble or masonry paviors were used for the floor, complemented by delft and coloured tiles on the walls, set off by an array of Wedgwood dairy porcelain, first introduced in 1770. If style was important, it would be added: the vaulted plaster ceiling and piscina in the dairy at Millearne by Richard Dickson creates an almost monastic atmosphere; whereas a fountain court in seventeenth century style, forms a setting for the dairy at Manderston.

Dairies tended to have three rooms or spaces: a churning room,

112

a scalding room, and a parlour. The churning room, at the heart of the dairy, would be furnished with a slate dresser round the walls, and a marble-topped table in the middle. There would be wooden pats to stamp the family crest upon the butter, heavy stone presses to produce cheese (which would be flavoured with mashed potato, oatmeal, mustard or caraway seeds according to the laird's taste), and other wooden utensils. An 1810 book condemned lead and copper utensils within the dairy as 'highly pernicious', whereas those of iron simply tasted bad. After 1800, barrel and box butter churns replaced traditional plunge churns.

Scalding rooms contained the copper for washing up; and the parlour was used for the sampling of produce. The early, ornamental dairy at Tombreac, Inveraray, exemplifies the problems in selecting a correct image. In 1753, John Adam had produced alternative, but classically-inspired designs for a number of small buildings linked by screen walls to pavilions. Behind them was a courtyard surrounded by byres, the swine to be 'fed out of a cistern, that shall be supplied from a spout from the Dairy'.[93] But since the dairy served, also, as an eyecatcher from the Castle, it had to be Gothicised. Bishop Pocock, in 1760, observed 'a building made to appear like a ruin, which is the dairy'. In 1787, the dairy was refurbished: 'the mock windows to be plaistered and painted to show as a window, one of the Turret windows that is in the Castle to be put in the middle part, and the wall to be straightened about it'.[94] Alterations followed in 1790 and 1794, when the central gable was raised and battlemented. Tombreac Dairy was demolished, or simply gave up the ghost, about 1880.

Venus Temple, on a hillock overlooking Taymouth Castle, was demolished in 1830 to make way for an elaborate, rustic dairy possibly designed by James Gillespie Graham.[95] Typically for Taymouth, their dairy went over the top: a large, two-storey building, with an exterior comprising several different materials: blue-stone, jagged shiny quartz, and rustic larch posts beneath a Welsh slate roof with larch-patterned eaves. The small leaded-light windows contained stained glass. Floors within of different coloured bricks and stones were laid in hexagonal patterns, and the walls, in cream Dutch tiles with a green border, rose to the stucco

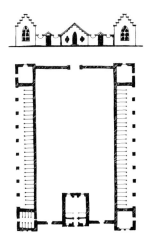

Tombreac dairy, Inveraray. One design in the turbulent life of this little structure.

113

Ground floor plan and west elevation from archive records of Taymouth dairy, and recent photograph of the structure.

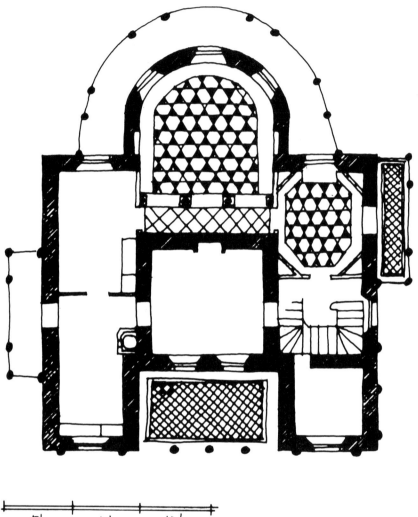

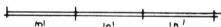

cornice above. The Breadalbane crest, in plaster relief, gazed from a vaulted ceiling. Hardly any of this detail was included in a mid-twentieth century 'restoration'.

An arcaded granite model dairy was instigated at Balmoral in 1861 along the lines of the one at Windsor. It is a delightful octagonal pavilion, surrounded by a crenellated arcade with a louvred roof surmounted by a leaded cupola, forming a dramatic frontage to the symmetrical farm buildings laid out behind it. The

114

The dairy at Balmoral, an arcaded essay in granite, was the idea of the Prince Consort.

dairy at Guisachan, by Glen Affric, has timber columns supporting a deep verandah in true rustic style. Geometric leaded lights of coloured glass allow sunlight to create patterns on the mosaic tiled floor within, centred upon a two-tier fountain.

There was a final flowering of model dairies at the start of the twentieth century. The marble and alabaster dairy at Manderston, by John Kinross, is an elaborate vaulted chamber joined to a tearoom in the neo-Baronial tower above a staircase. The model dairy at Borgue, 1901, is a Gothick converted 'palace' around the central tower, a baronial structure intended as a water tower yet found to be useless on completion; legend has it that twelve cows were tethered there with chains of silver. William Flockart's 1907 dairy at Rosehaugh, Black Isle, was modelled on one at Sandringham. With its gambrel-roof of peg tiles, it is a good example of the English vernacular revival in Scotland. One of the last dairies to be built was also the most distinctive; Sir Robert Lorimer's dairy at Kinfauns Castle, Home Farm near Perth, completed in 1922. It is an ogee-roofed pavilion surrounded by a continuous verandah, and linked to a small Dutch-gabled scullery.

Game Larders

It seems likely that storage of game began by burying it in game pits. One such pit lies adjacent to the restored icehouse at Colzium, and consists of a chamber two metres deep, tapering outwards from seventy centimetres diameter at ground level, to a metre at the bottom. It would have been used to store the carcasses of hares, rabbits, pheasants and partridges; less so venison, which was liable to become tainted if buried too long, and had to be spotted with saltpetre. It was clearly much more hygienic to hang game in a game larder.

However, few game larders appear to have been built before 1830, and the rapid increase in their numbers after 1850 coincides with the growth of sporting estates and popularity of deer stalking and grouse shooting. The most important attributes of the game larder were shade (achieved by wide eaves), ventilation (adjusted by louvres and underfloor vents), and security from vermin and insects (best achieved with fly screens, and raising the larder some distance from the ground). One chamber was frequently placed concentrically within another.

The Abbotsford game larder, built into an earth bank below the terrace, consists of a series of rooms including one in which a large timber hanging-frame, beset with hooks, is let into the brick vault, its crown a vent in the terrace above. Gargoyles guard the external turnpike stair which winds up to the terrace, from which there are fine views over parkland to the Tweed. The battlemented game larder 'tower' at Raith has nine checked, vertical slits in its ashlar walls doubling as imitation arrow loops, and yet providing plentiful airflow while blocking direct sunlight. It also boasts a viewing platform, reached by an internal turnpike stair, which overlooks an ornamental steading and limpid pool. The plinth on which the larder sits is reputed to contain an icehouse.

In 1860, the Prince Consort was largely responsible for the construction of an elegant, harled circular game larder at Balmoral, which now forms part of a group. Decorated with a frieze of stags' heads and pierced with arrow slit vents, it is capped by a conical slate roof surmounted by a louvred lantern. Few other game larders

116

DECORATIVE LARDERS

The gamelarder at Fyvie. Lighter than masonry, the timber construction offers plenty of shade and ventilation.

At House of Dun, the gamelarder, elevated on a single post, stands at the centre of a courtyard.

achieved such decorative potential.

In the later nineteenth century, cheaper prefabricated, often timber-framed game larders superseded masonry construction, since they could be relocated quite easily. Of the timber varieties, perhaps the most attractive survivor is that at the House of Dun: a slatted pavilion supported on a single central post, linked to the ground by five timber steps. The leaded roof above is gathered up into an ogee-shape. It rests in the shade of a circle of trees at the centre of the courtyard buildings, which now include a gamekeeper's room, potting shed, loom and yarn room, two coach-houses, and a tea-room. The property is now in the care of the National Trust for Scotland.

Freshwater Fish ponds

The 'P' shaped depression of a medieval fishpond which can still be traced below the southern walls of Craigmillar Castle symbolises the long history and importance of fish farming. However, by its very nature, it seems to have left few buildings behind. In 1685, John James recommended the inclusion of deep fishponds as features within walled gardens, and there is some evidence that they continued to be formed throughout the eighteenth century. In his memoirs, Sir John Clerk recorded that he stocked his own fishponds at Penicuik with carp and tench sent all the way from Corby Castle. However, he also explained the other uses of the fishpond: 'I have various fishponds, and one especially which forms a lake rather than a pond. It is situated in the midst of a wood which is dissected by a number of paths. Four little islands, covered with shrubs, adorn it, and afford hiding places for ducks and aquatic birds of the sort. It supports a great multitude of fish which, either from natural joy or with the desire of catching flies, are seen continually to skip and play and throw themselves about. Here, therefore, for walking, or fishing, or hunting, my whole family at time take exercise'.[96] It seems probable that perch, which in 1653 Izaak Walton called 'so wholesome that physicians allow him to be eaten by wounded men', and pike, 'a dish of meat too good for any but anglers or very honest men' would have formed the principal stock of freshwater fishponds. They are certainly central to many recipes, many of which required herbs and vinegar.[97]

The symbolic importance of fish may be inferred from the structure with which Sir William Bruce graced the loch 'full of the finest Trouts in the World': Loch Leven, as described by John Macky. The east vista from Kinross House to Loch Leven Castle is framed by the Fish Gate, an elaborately carved construction by stonemasons Peter Paul Boyce and Cornelius van Neerven. A relief carving of a basket of the seven varieties of Loch Leven fish – carp, bream, perch, pike, catfish, bool trout and red trout – is flanked on either side by rusticated gate-piers topped by statues of a boy riding a dolphin.

During the later eighteenth and nineteenth centuries, many original fishponds were expanded into serpentine lakes, integral to the new romantic landscape designs.

Saltwater Fishponds

Coastal estates farmed both fresh and saltwater reserves. Hopetoun House had an oyster bed overlooked by a terrace, statue walk and a pheasant house. A saltwater pond was created at Inveraray in 1752, controlled and freshened by a special sluice. It was stocked with 900 oysters, but soon proved vulnerable to high tides, which flooded it with mud. The construction of the new coast road in 1757 cut the pond from the sea, and thus it ceased; the celebrated Loch Fyne oysters of nowadays are farmed in easier circumstances. The most interesting example of such fishponds that can be seen today is that at Logan House, near Stranraer. It is possible for visitors to hand feed the fish that are still kept in the natural, saltwater pond formed from the living rock. Modified in 1800, the pond was given an enclosing wall and a Gothick keeper's cottage. Some ten metres deep, the pond is a natural fish larder, linked to sea by means of a grille. Occupants have included pollack, wrasse, and plaice: the present tenants are cod.

Birds

Birds have long been a source of meat, dung, oil and eggs in Scotland. They were also, on occasion, kept for decoration and for hunting. Pigeons were reputed to possess medicinal qualities, and

119

became the focus of superstition in the seventeenth century. Young pigeons 'cloven through the middle' and applied to the chest, were used to comfort the heart, as recommended by James Primrose in 1638. Fifty years later, Francis Willoughby recommended 'a live pigeon cut asunder along the backbone and clapped on the head for mitigating fierce humours and a melancholy sadness. Hence it is a most proper medicine in the plurisie, headache, melancholy and gout. . . . ' and a source of 'new life and vigour'. Pigeon dung mixed with bear's grease, pepper and oil of cumin was even recommended for baldness.

Birds of prey were bred for falconry, and used on heron ponds at Hatton House, and Dawyck – a favourite hunting location for James I. Birds kept in an aviary for decorative purposes seem to have permeated Scotland quite early. Sir John Clerk was the proud possessor of one such: 'Among other gardens there is one, or rather an aviary, near the window of my chamber where sometimes I feed the various birds with my hand. Here ducks, Guinea fowls, partridges and occasionally pheasants daily look for my help'.[98] In 1762, Bishop Forbes noted 'a little castle upon an eminence, mounted with some small cannon and having a spiral walk up to it' at Dunkeld. In the grounds were different kinds of pheasant 'with their chicks, patridges and turtle doves'.[99] The best collection of bird-buildings probably survives at Culzean; an 1882 Gothick goose house on an island in the thirteen-acre Swan Pond. An aviary, built as a copy of the 'pheasantry' illustrated in R Lugar's *Plans and Views of Building, 1811*, forms a little courtyard; and the 1860 Chinese Pagoda had a tea-room overlooking the swans' pens. Although there were proposals on other estates for ornamental aviaries fronting reflecting pools, such structures were not common.

In general, the importance of the birds was for eating. The fondness of natives for the gannets and kittywakes from the Bass Rock did not commend itself to Daniel Defoe: 'a very course dish, rank and ill-relished, and soon gorging the stomach'.[100] Cranes were larded, roasted and eaten with ginger. Birds were stewed with raisins in a spicy broth, and peacocks were served 'in hackle' (in their skin and feathers). Pigeons from the doocots were rolled in paste and boiled as dumplings, baked in pots with claret and sealed with butter to keep for three months, or 'transmogrified' (tucked inside a large hollowed cucumber, legs one end and the head the other, with a bunch of barberries in the bill for decoration).

'Squab pie' made with a twice-baked crust, was popular. Birds were also made into salami, stuffed with garlic or even 'arranged in the form of a spider . . . a frog . . . or in the form of the moon'. Birds as food were far more important than birds as decoration: and the most significant structure for birds was the doocot.

Doocots

Doocots were reserves of food available to the laird and his family throughout the year. They were popular because they needed little maintenance, and pigeons readily took to them. The birds were caught in nets, or shutters drawn across the pigeon ports to prevent escape. Gourmets preferred to eat flightless young birds, only a few weeks old (called squabs or peesers), which, it was recommended, should be force-fed with water-soaked Indian grain. Eggs were gathered from nesting boxes by means of a revolving ladder or potence, with rungs on brackets suspended from a central pole or arbre. When a new doocot was completed, pigeons were lured to take up residence with bait such as 'salt cat'—grain flavoured with cumin, old wine or myrrh (great sweet garden chervil). In elaborate estates, other comforts were provided: the doocot at Ravelston, Edinburgh has a stone bird bath. The floor of the doocot provided copious quantities of rich fertilising pigeon dung which, flailed to a fine powder, was cast upon fields as fertiliser. It was also used in leather tanning and cloth dyeing, and its high potassium nitrate content made it suitable for the manufacture of gunpowder, when mixed with black earth and sulphur.[101]

It is not clear how old the doocot is. At the Bronze Age settlement of Skara Brae on Orkney, there is a structure which may have been an early doocot. The Romans built them, although none are known to have survived in Scotland, and perhaps the earliest are the coastal 'doo caves' like those below Macduff's castle at West Wemyss in Fife, or at Dunglass.

Doocots became the legal right of abbeys, baronies, castles and monasteries; and statutory protection of doocots had become neces-

In 1776 a number of designs were prepared by Robert Mylne to convert Carloonan doocot into a temple with the addition of an arcade; none of these were realised. (Royal Commission on Ancient Monuments, Scotland.)

Frontage dated 1874 to the offices at Edrom Mains, with a doocot above the pend.

sary as early as 1424, as the birds' appetite for the peasants' crops led to resentment and revenge. Destroyers of pigeon houses could expect to be fined as severely as the 'stealers of green wood by night', or the 'peelers of bark to the destruction of the trees'. From 1503, parents were required to accept responsibility and a fine for children who broke into pigeon houses; the child itself would be flogged. By 1567, shooting of the laird's pigeons risked a forty-day sentence, with the loss of one's right hand on a second conviction. By the end of the sixteenth century, repeated offences against pigeons carried the death penalty. By 1603 legislation compelled 'ilk, Lord and Laird to make them dowecots', and in general, a doocot can be taken as sometimes the only surviving sign of an ancient tower or house. By 1617, doocot building had become so popular that a licence to build one was only available to lairds whose land produced an annual turnover of at least ten chalders of grain.

Doocot building continued through the seventeenth and eigh-

Pies have been popular from at least as long ago as the Middle Ages. One suggestion is that the word has associations with 'magpies', the link being a predeliction for collecting assorted ingredients. A double-crust or twice-baked pie was a particularly filling example and a good way to eat older and tougher birds.

Take 4–6 pigeons; dress and joint them. Prepare gravy by simmering the backs and necks with 4 cloves, salt and pepper. At the base of a well-greased pie dish place either a bay leaf or a little shredded shallot or garlic. Cover with a slice of scored raw beef and lay on this the pigeon pieces. Season well. Add 6 small mushrooms together with diced bacon trimmings or scraps from a ham bone. Fill up with half of the spiced gravy and cover with a thin suet crust which should lie down on the meat inside the pie dish. Cover with a lid and bake for about one hour until this crust is thoroughly cooked and as light as bread.

Remove from the oven. Cut the dumpling crust into squares and pack it down amongst the tender cooked meat. Fill the dish with the balance of the hot gravy. As an alternative to cutting the suet crust, it can simply be submerged by adding more mushrooms, hard-boiled eggs quartered, fruit, or any quickly cooked filling. Cover with a light shortcrust pastry top and bake for a further 25 minutes until crisp and brown. To serve, cut a slice from the top crust and lift out a square of the 'huff pastry' (the dumpling paste). On it arrange a pigeon on its piece of beef, and surround this with mushrooms, bacon trimmings, gravy and so on. Top off with the slice of pie crust. It seems that it was traditional to embed 4 pigeon feet in the top crust but this custom seems to have died out in the middle of the nineteenth century.

teenth centuries, thereafter, the structures were more generally incorporated into the cupolas, towers and pediments of farm steadings. But the birds grew very unpopular. In 1796, it was estimated that Midlothian pigeons swallowed enough grain to feed three thousand people, and that some thirty-six thousand pairs of breeding birds were resident in nesting boxes in Fife alone. They were the prime beneficiaries of the success of agricultural improvements. Yet improvements in animal husbandry reduced the dependence on pigeons for winter meat. Hens provided bigger eggs, and farmyard dung was at least as good and far more plentiful, than could be obtained from the doocot. The disadvantage of pigeons had begun to outweigh the advantages, and after the early nineteenth century, few were built outside steadings.

The buildings did not become redundant in the nineteenth century; merely less important functionally and visually. They changed in character and context from important buildings to be

Interior of the beehive doocot at West Meikle Pinkerton. Rows of stone nesting boxes filled the circular interior, reached by crawling through the low door.

seen in pleasure grounds, to a functional part of the domestic offices. Some were converted: as early as 1776, Robert Mylne proposed to convert the Carloonan doocot to an arcaded temple;[102] that at Bonnington House was converted to a moss house, at Mellerstain to a cottage ornée, and some were even used as corn drying kilns. The Stow doocot became a bothy for navvies building the Edinburgh to Galashiels road, and Sir Robert Lorimer converted the 1694 doocot at Mounie Castle into a garden house. The doocot at Loretto School, Edinburgh was converted to a memorial tower for a deceased headmaster.

The only significant doocots to have been constructed after about 1850 appear to have been those set on the edge of croquet lawns and terraces of Edwardian mansions. The occupants were not so much pigeons, as doves kept for decorative reasons – for example, white fantails which may occasionally have been coloured with vegetable dye to mark special occasions. These doocots are tiny shelters, sometimes occupying the roof space of a croquet pavilion, or a little void in a garden wall. Sir Robert Lorimer probably designed the small timber 'fuie' fixed to the garden wall at Kellie Castle. The doocot at Crathes was removed and repositioned in 1935 to act as a focal point in one corner of the decorative garden.

The original function of the doocot to provide food is now wholly obsolete; but many of them still act as safe houses or hotels for feral pigeons. The doocots at Muiravonside and Boath have both been restored, the latter by the National Trust for Scotland: it stands within a much earlier earth work—the remains of the twelfth century Castle of Eren. That at Tealing is a scheduled Ancient Monument, while the example at nearby Finavon now houses a doocot museum. At least one large doocot has become a tiny human house: but such conversion inevitably requires the destruction of nesting boxes and the formation of unnaturally large windows to the ruination of the original character of the building.

Beehive Doocots

The name 'beehive' derives from the resemblance of these older-fashioned doocots to straw bee-skeps. Their main characteristic is a rotund massivity, surmounted by a shallow domed roof supporting a central cupola or 'glover' which allows pigeons to enter and leave whilst offering some protection from swooping hawks. The circular stone walls are raised usually in three or four stages, each marked with a rat course or projecting ledge, to deter climbing vermin. A small, and often heavily fortified door led the egg gatherer into a single chamber, lined on all sides with rows of square nesting boxes. A large doocot could contain five hundred of them, usually in squared rubble or dressed stone, one for each pair of nesting birds. Most of these early doocots have a ponderous quality, if a certain unsophisticated charm. What little ornament there may be, is usually restricted to a billet-moulded cornice. A number seem to have been elaborated at later dates to provide either greater elegance, or improved accommodation.

Early examples of beehive doocots may be found in the defensive

At Crossraguel the doocot is built into the abbey walls.

walls of Crossraguel Abbey and Dirleton Castle, or within the policies of towers such as Newark, Dunure, and Aberdour Castles. Of this type of doocot, perhaps the most unusual but best known example is that at Phantassie, East Linton, now owned by the National Trust for Scotland.

Lectern Doocots

As the name implies, lectern doocots were in the shape of a lectern: rectangular, with a cut-away, mono-pitch roof.[103] In 1819, the Poet Laureate, Robert Southey, accurately described them as being like 'the section of a house cut in half'. They were not only simple to build, but also lent themselves to far greater architectural pretension than the beehive doocots, which they began to replace by the late sixteenth century.

The interior of the lectern doocot was normally divided into two separate chambers, although occasionally, as at Leitcheston, into four. Each would be lined, full height, with nesting boxes. Really grand versions could accommodate more than 2,500 pairs of nesting birds, but they tended to be located in areas of richer agricultural land. Since the separation of the chambers meant fewer disturbances from egg gatherers, greater security from thieves, vermin and disease, each chamber normally had its own door. Additional security was rare, but took the form of double doors as at Waterybutts, near Errol, and a moat at Careston. Occasionally, it was sufficient to 'plant the pigeon house in the middle of the court-yard and near enough to the house, that the master of the family may keep in awe those who go in or come out'. Whether to deter thieves or not, access to the second chamber at Dalmahoy is reached below a false floor in the first.

One of the earliest lectern doocots, dating from the sixteenth century, survives beside Tantallon Castle, with no other architectural embellishment upon its plain, strong, form save crow-step gables. Lectern doocots offered considerably greater opportunity for embellishment than the beehive because the form was so architectural. Rat courses became elegant string courses, stepping up and down on the elevation, embracing heraldic devices and armorial panels. The vocabulary extended to include sundials, ball finials,

Phantassie doocot is basically of beehive type, but the north wall has been extended upward to form a sunny monopitched roof.

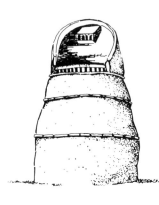

126

The lectern doocot at Glamis is twin chambered, with an unusual raised north wall providing shelter and extra perching space.

carved heads, incised panels and, later, cusped carved parapets, crenellated gables, dummy windows, dormer windows, and highly decorated pigeon ports which could be fitted with shutters, and closed by levers from outside. Lead model pigeons, wings outspread, presumably as lures, decorate the skews of the large 2140-nest doocot at Johnstounburn. The subdivision into chambers within is effected by means of a large masonry cylinder, itself lined with nesting boxes.

Sometimes, doocots were created by fitting wooden nesting boxes into the relics of older structures, and the results can be curious. The crossing tower of Dunbar's Blackfriars monastery is thus preserved, as is a medieval chapel by Lundin Tower, Fife. It was also a favourite use for the tapered towers of disused mills, as at Melville Castle and Schaw Park, and for surviving stair towers of demolished houses— as at Dunipace and Edmondston.

127

Drumquhassle doocot dated 1711 is single chambered, with crowsteps that terminate in columns capped with ball finials.

Pavilion Doocots

In the eighteenth and nineteenth centuries, doocots took on distinct architectural form in keeping with other pavilions in the landscape. There was an increase in self-conscious designs, and some rose to become significant architectural statements, small scale experiments by designers keen to try their hand at something new. Most, however, were no more than reasonably prestigious estate buildings, in an age that cared about such things.

That the new pavilion doocots were usually two-storey in height was about all they had in common. They could be square, circular,

128

hexagonal, octagonal and even pentagonal. Some were harled, some built in ashlar, some decorated with niches, others with pilasters, and the roofs took whatever form their owner or architect fancied – conical, pyramids, cupolas, weather-vanes, lanterns and turrets.

The majority of these decorative doocots raised the nesting boxes to first floor level and above; which created higher and more dynamically massed structures and left the ground floor for other uses. These could be donkey shed, wine cellar, potting shed, feed boiling room, store, icehouse as at Bowbutts and Murdostoun; dairy or tea-house as at Invermay; and even a burial vault as at Stroma (in which a number of travellers record witnessing the mummifying of human bodies with some horrid tales). Dishan Tower, near Balfour House on Shapinsay, has the unlikely combination of pigeon-house and salt-water shower; the Italianate campanile at Luffness served both as doocot and water tower; and the slate-roofed arcade beneath the Fothringham doocot shelters a cattle shed.

In 1748, Roger Morris completed a harled, circular doocot at Carloonan at Inveraray, 'to be built at the end of the Oak Walk, being a circular building twenty foot diameter and forty-two foot high, to stand up on a slope three foot high'. By comparison with what was to follow, it was fairly plain. In the same year, Sir John Clerk commenced the construction of Terregles Tower at Penicuik. Three storeys in height, with a machicolated parapet at the head of a turnpike stair, the tower contained nearly 1500 nesting boxes for pigeons. Although unusual, it was quite overshadowed by Clerk's second doocot, built some twelve years later in the court of offices. It was described thus by Sir Walter Scott in *Waverley*: 'A ton-bellied pigeon-house of great size and rotundity, resembling in figure and proportion the curious edifice called Arthur's Oven, which would have turned the brains of all the antiquaries in England, had not the worthy proprietor pulled it down for the sake of mending a neighbouring dam-dyke'. Arthur's O'on had been built as the Roman Temple of Terminus on the banks of the River Carron at Stenhouse. Clerk was able to use measured drawings made before its destruction in 1743, and justified his reproduction of it in the block at Penicuik thus: 'I propose an ornament to the country by it. I likewise have in mind to make it beneficial to my family . . . (the

Proposal at Polmaise by Daniel Mathie, 1786, for a doocot at the centre of a courtyard measuring 110' by 62' 6".

Lead pigeons, wings outstretched, poised to fly from the skews at Johnstounburn.

doocot) which I have by the House being hurt by too many trees where Hawks and Gleds destroy the pigeons when they come out'.[104]

A number of the large, plain, cylindrical doocots still survive, that at Daldowie one of the best examples with its ogee-slated roof. Architectural motifs such as sculptured niches appear in the walls of the pink ashlar doocot at Strathleven House, while the doocot at Nisbet Hill is a pentagonal pavilion with a stone slate roof rising to a large ball finial. It was probably more common to have doocots in the romantic manner. A square doocot at Saltoun Hall has a crenellated octagonal turret; Mounthooly also a crenellated parapet with twelve ball finials; and the 1770 pavilion in Pittencreiff Park, Dunfermline, a round crenellated tower. The arcaded doocot, com-

Opposite
At Colstoun House the cylindrical eighteenth century doocot was once freestanding but it was absorbed into later farm offices.

Kinross doocot forms a slender and elegant centrepiece to the quadrangle commenced in 1690.

Denbie doocot, containing some 250 nesting boxes of brick and dressed stone, bears the datestone 'JC 1775'.

131

The doocot at Nisbet Hill of possibly unique pentagonal plan, is finished with a stone slate roof terminating in a ball finial.

Particularly fine example of a mid-eighteenth century pavilion doocot at Huntington (RCAHMS).

Proposal for a doocot 38 feet high at Whim by William Adam and Lord Milton, circa 1740, when pleasure grounds were being laid out around the house.

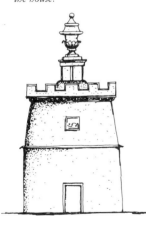

plete with dummy windows centred in the charming courtyard, at Megginch,[105] reflects the Gothick taste with ornamental arrow-slits, and *quatrefoil* decoration. Three early nineteenth century doocots at Inverquhomery are also Gothick, while that at the House of Pitmuies has towers with glazed cruciform windows, datestone and armorial panels.

The 1750 doocot at Huntington is not only the finest in the Lothians, but the epitome of the pavilion doocot. It is designed like a miniature temple: the upper storey, pedimented, finialed, pilastered sitting above a plain plinth. It has a graciousness and quality astounding for a doocot, and well worthy of being a tea or summer house.

The doocot at House of Pitmuies.

133

Chatelherault, now open to the public. Illustrating its principle elevation in 'Vitruvius Scoticus', the designer William Adam termed it 'The Dogg Kennell'. (Photo by Charles McKean.)

Chapter 5

Landscape with Buildings

The new romanticism of the eighteenth century implied that the beauties of the estate would unfold themselves to visitors as they were driven from the gate-house to the mansion. There would be carefully planned, alluring and oblique glimpses of the house itself, its court of offices, its stables, or its walled gardens. The drive would be punctuated by bridges or woods, and there would be the occasional glimpse of little temples, other pavilions and views over the lake to the hills beyond. Since the purpose was to convince the visitor that his host's policies were limitless, walls that might be mistakenly read as boundaries were minimised or removed; replaced as necessary to control the movement of stock by ha-has (invisible sunken walls). Few of those glimpsed temples and pavilions had a seriously functional purpose. Only the largest provided sleeping accommodation or anything in the way of shelter for either visitors or workers. They were built for pleasure and diversion; and there was a clear difference between those designed to impress or brag from a long distance, and those whose task was rather to beckon or thrill.

The most distinguished survivor is the Duke of Hamilton's hunting lodge at Chatelherault, near Hamilton, designed by William Adam between 1732–42 for the Duke of Hamilton, named after their title of Chatelherault in France. This extraordinary development functions on several levels. The eastern pavilions front the courtyard which provided space for kennels for hunting dogs and associated service buildings; the western contained the magnificent banqueting house, and retiring rooms for the Duke and Duchess. Within the formal garden, was a small pavilion built as a menagerie, once alleged to have contained baboons, a leopard, wolves, an eagle, and 'munkies'; but seemingly large enough to contain only one of them. Its other purpose was to impress those

The summerhouse at Dunglass dated 1718, is distinguished with a fine carved frieze of ram's heads and flowers. It is situated on high ground beside artificial earthworks which seem to have included a bowling green.

Opposite
Apollo's Temple at Taymouth may predate mid eighteenth century proposals for landscaping the park, and there have been hints of some connection between this building and 'faerie rites'.

visiting the Duke in the great palace of Hamilton, a mile downhill in the Clyde Valley. From that distance it would have appeared, as it appears today, as the skyline of a Baroque fortress, punctuated by four, tall, pedimented pavilions in two pairs, linked by a single storey screen wall with urns, ball finials, and blind, baroque gun ports.

Rescued from utter dereliction by architects Boys Jarvis, Chatelherault has been restored, complete with its formal gardens and parterre. The interior of the banqueting house is even more splendid than its exterior: a long, high, marble-flagged room with magnificent plasterwork on the ceiling, cornice and walls carefully recreated by Dick Reid. Unless or until the Great Garden of the Earl of Mar at Alloa is restored, Chatelherault will provide Scotland with

The Temple of Pomona at Cullen which was equipped with a form of underfloor heating.

its finest evocation of a late Baroque design. The location of this magnificence is on the banks of the ravine of the River Avon, on the other side from the ruins of Cadzow Castle, ancient seat of the Hamiltons; and behind which stretch the High Parks, relict of the ancient Caledonian forest with its wild, horned white cattle. Chatelherault has been restored as a country park and interpretation centre, and now incorporates possibly the only baroque adventure playground in Scotland.

Most early eighteenth century pavilions of a simpler sort harked back to the antique form of a temple (almost irrespective of what their actual use might be). Their popularity may be guessed from the variety of designs in the classic style contained in James Gibb's 1728 *Book of Architecture*. In the early part of the century, they were placed formally at the intersection of paths to close the vistas, or to emphasise a particular point in the route around the estate; and were almost certainly used as summer houses, offering secluded retreats 'from the fatigues of a sultry day'.[106]

Queen Mary's Bath House, Edinburgh, may never have been a bath house at all.

A particularly ornate hexagonal 1718 summer house at Dunglass has an elaborately carved dark red sandstone frieze of swags, flowers, and a ram's head. Its slated, ogee-roof is gathered up into an enormous leaded ball. In 1783, William Adam designed a belvedere for the Countess of Eglington at her estate near Irvine in the form of a solid, round, domed drum, enclosed by an Ionic colonnade. Adam's now ruinous two-storey Island Temple by the River Deveron at Duff House, Banff was designed in 1738 for Lord Braco to mark the climax to the charming walk along the river from the picturesque bridge of Alvah.[107] It might also have been used as a fishing pavilion. The Temple of Fame, erected above Diana's Grove[108] at Blair in 1745, contained two tiers of busts of those entitled to such immortality. They included Saturn, Venus, Cicero and Plato with the ancients, and Shakespeare and Newton amongst the moderns. No contemporary political figures were thought up to it. In 1759, Charles Hope-Weir added a circular temple with a Doric portico to the top of Leny Hill, at his seat of Craigiehall. It contained fine plasterwork until first destroyed by fire, then vandalised in the 1960s, before the top floor was unceremoniously lopped off for an extension to Edinburgh Airport in 1975.

How these temples looked, redolent as they were of ancient mysteries, was considerably more important than how they functioned. The rotunda erected by Sir William Chambers in Duddingston House in 1768 was intended to be viewed axially, from which viewpoint it appeared to be sitting upon only four columns. However, when viewed obliquely, it can be seen that the rotunda's dome is supported by eight. The Temple of Pomona (or Fame) at Cullen, possibly based on James Playfair's 1788 design, is one of the most sophisticated. Eventually built by William Robertson in 1822 on a bluff overlooking Cullen Bay, it comprises a domed rotunda supported on eight Ionic columns which enclosed a statue within. A panelled room equipped with underfloor heating is contained inside the plinth.

When next you explore a derelict estate, and chance upon a bosky circle of columns supporting a dome, the chances are that this was the spot that some peruked Prince thought that he might meet the goddess Diana: and maybe he did.

Tea-Houses

The mysterious pavilion might, alternatively, have been where the laird and his guests gathered to take tea. Tea was a cult for the landed classes in early eighteenth century Scotland (although regarded unsuitable for lower orders since it provided 'gratification without nourishment'). Tea pavilions, like an aggrandised summer house, were sometimes built to a scale sufficient for holding small banquets. The finest of those is undoubtedly Oswald's Temple at Auchincruive, near Ayr, designed in 1778 by Robert Adam for Richard Oswald, a London merchant. It was modelled on the mausoleum of the Emperor Theodoric at Ravenna, which Adam had visited in 1755, and is tall, elegant, and circular. Originally a double-raked stair led to a tea-room and terrace on the principal floor; kitchen, pantry, store, closet and wine cellar below. Something similar was designed by James Adam for Balbardie House near Bathgate in 1793 (now demolished).

Bath House

If that classical temple were set beside a stream, it might represent an eighteenth century bath house. Baths were not in great demand in pre-Victorian Scotland, although occasionally an aristocrat would buck the smelly trend, and decide to wash. The sixteenth century tower known as Queen Mary's Bath House by Holyrood Palace, Edinburgh is more likely to have been built as a pavilion connected with nearby tennis courts; but bath houses certainly existed at the time. One was built into the ornate garden walls of Edzell Castle in 1604. Its foundations clearly show three apartments, presumably a bathroom, dressing room and sitting room. Since the bath house set into the seventeenth century wall linking twin gazebos at Hatton is not shown in the contemporaneous engraving by John Slezer, it must clearly be a later addition. The Hatton bath is a circular basin some three metres in diameter and over a metre deep, something like the dimensions of a jacuzzi. It had a tessellated pavement, and its vaulted ceiling was formerly encrusted with shells. Water was fed into the bath from a font in the walls, its source being the basin of an ornamental fountain in the terrace above.

140

The Round House on the beach at Culzean, just beside the bath house.

Clare Hall, a visionary Neo-classical project by Sir John Clerk intended to combine a lakeside bathhouse at Penicuik with an elaborate library. (Courtesy of Sir John Clerk of Penicuik.)

The 1830 bath house at Pitfour is in the form of a Temple to Theseus standing beside the artificial lake. (Royal Commission on Ancient Monuments, Scotland.)

The pavilion containing a bath house would ordinarily be set in the bank of a stream or loch to ensure a sufficient source of water. It would consist of a plunge pool and another, heated chamber, presumably for robing and disrobing. Walls would be decorated with tiles and sculpture of a suitable bathing theme. Drawings for bath houses by the Adam family, like those in contemporary pattern books such as the *Gentlemen and Farmers' Architect*, 1762, reveal a preference for little domed buildings dignified by a pedimented doorway. A late eighteenth century bath house on the shore at Culzean is accompanied by a nearby round house, *circa* 1800, constructed evidently as a changing room (but whether for sea bathing

142

or for the bath house is unclear). A much larger building at Penicuik House, proposed for a site beside an ornamental lake, owed not a little to the Pantheon. Titled Clare Hall, it would have combined hot water baths and a cold plunge at a lower level, with the experience of ascending a majestic staircase into the great, domed, vaulted library above. There, seated in sybaritic comfort, the visitor could contemplate volumes of the classics, collections of pattern books, documents, and other souvenirs of his education at Leyden, and the subsequent Grand Tour, which Sir John Clerk would undoubtedly have kept there. The sadly derelict lakeside bath house at Pifour, 1830, took the form of a Temple to Theseus. Granite columns support a wooden entablature, and a rectangular plunge pool is cut into the masonry plinth within.

Pump House

If that neglected ruin were not a bath house, it might be the even rarer structure that was erected for medicinal purposes to take the waters – the pump house. One was built in 1760 at Inveraray around a mineral well of 'steel and sulphur'. The style was four-arched Gothick, to which it was proposed to add further decoration and a spire. The best accessible example of the mineral well is St Bernard's Well, by the Water of Leith within Edinburgh. The juxtaposition of a pure classical temple against the wild landscape was one particularly sought after by eighteenth century painters and landscapists; and it reached its apogee in this building. Built by Alexander Nasmyth for Lord Gardenstone in 1789, the well takes the form of an elegant, Doric rotunda. The statue of Hygeia was installed in 1888. The mineral spring which it celebrated was described by Robert Forsyth in 1805 as 'having a slight resemblance in flavour to the washings of a foul gunbarrel'. Restoration of the well is complete, and it is open to the public at weekends.

Mid-century taste for novelty encouraged many forms of exotic design: Hindoo, Icelandic, Egyptian, and above all the Chinese style favoured by Sir William Chambers and Robert Adam.[109] In 1755, there were proposals to erect a Chinese temple in the gardens at Dunkeld, possibly in competition with the Chinese tent, equipped with gilded bells, dragons, spiral ornament, and blue, yellow and

*View of St Bernard's Well,
Edinburgh, from a lithograph
by J D Harding after W L
Leitch circa 1854 (Central
Library, Edinburgh).*

*Elevation by Roger Morris,
1753, of a Chinese Temple
proposed for Dunkeld House.
(From His Grace the Duke of
Atholl's Collection.)*

vermilion paint, which the estate accounts of nearby Taymouth show to have been erected in the previous year. There are few survivors of this eighteenth century obsession with the Orient.

Rustic Buildings and Hermitages

The reverse image of the uplifting glory of the temple was the romantic chasm and ghastly grotto: both formed an integral part of the experience of an enlightened estate. It was the fashion to appreciate, as a substance of the sublime, nature's more dramatic enterprises – the roaring rocky gorge, leafy glen, majestic waterfall, or moist, dripping, fern-strewn river bed. Whether at Glen Tilt, Gifford Water, the Humble Bumble at Invermay, or the Black and White Lochs at Castle Kennedy, a cathartic experience could be offered. Man's embellishment of such spots consisted of sympathetically primitive grottos, caves, hermitages and summer houses, their principal characteristic being the sophisticated use of naturally-occurring materials in their raw state. To enhance the atmosphere, the texture would express extremes: of hardness and brittleness (the palate of the sublime) or of softness and pliability (the palate of the picturesque). Favoured materials included rough timber, flint, glass, sharp glistening crystalline quartz, large shells, patterns of small shells, and tufa – a volcanic relative of pumice which arrived in Scotland as ship's ballast from Iceland. If grotesquely weathered sandstone could be carved from the cliffs, so much the better. Rusticated masonry would be used for the entrance to the grotto, and for the tunnel, and sometimes for little bridges that spanned white, foaming water in picturesque gorges.

Tunnels and Grottos

Artificial grottos were intended to heighten man's experience and to inculcate a sense of awe. The earliest surviving grotto in Scotland is William Adam's 1726 man-made tunnel with formal pedimented entry at Arniston, which leads to a secluded retreat overlooking a rushing stream. Noise of the water is reflected back against an arena of unhewn rocks studded with niches and seats (and a date-stone of 1644 possibly from Edinburgh's Parliament House). Adam is also attributed with the design of the 1747 rusticated grotto built around

The grotto at Bealachanuaran, Inverarary, celebrates the source of a hillside spring.

the springhead of Bealachanuaran, a particularly romantic spot in the woods beside Inveraray Castle, (and the site of the lovers' first tryst in Neil Munro's *John Splendid*). It takes the form of a little pedimented temple with ball finials focused on a large, heavily rusticated entrance. The plain chamber within contains the springhead.

In 1742, Sir John Clerk constructed Hurleycove Tunnel as a Scots version of the Grotto of Pausalipo at Naples. He described it thus:

> It is surrounded by hills and steep rocks, and no one can get access to it but by the mouth of a frightful cave. To those who enter, therefore, first occurs the memory of the Cave of the Cuman Sibyl, for the ruinous aperture, blocked up with stones and briars, strikes the eye. Then there comes upon the wayfarers a shudder, as they stand in doubt whether they are among the living or the dead. As, indeed, certain discords set off and give finish to musical cadencies in such a way as to render the subsequent harmony more grateful to the ear, so does the form of this mournful cave,[110] with its long shady path followed by the light and prospect, make the exit more

*Inside the former Hermitage
above the Falls of Acharn.
Recent treefelling has reduced
the romance and melodrama
of this spot.*

delightful. For suddenly the darkness disappears, as it were at
the creation of a new world. . . . [111]

One hundred and forty seven feet long from its gate to the side of
the lake at the far end, the tunnel is punctuated mid-way by a little
chamber with a stone bench and the inscription *Tenebrosa Ocultaque
Cave*—an admonition to 'Beware of what is dark and hidden'. Sir
John continued to enjoy daily 'my constant walk to my pond of
Hurley and Grotto, where I take great delight'[112] up to his old age.
On an early November morning, so it is said, the sun shines right
through the tunnel to the haugh on the far side. It was argued that
the tunnel also served the functional purpose of a scientific instru-
ment to 'determine the diameter of the sun's body, provided it was
closed at both ends with doors, in which glasses might be fitted as
for a telescope of the same length'.[113] At the south end of the tunnel,
was a summer house with kitchen and dining room.[114]

Two tunnels, one of twenty and another of thirty metres long,
were created on the riverside walk in the grounds of Dalkeith
Palace. The shorter is serpentine with a mid-point chamber which

147

opens sheer above the rushing river below. The far end debouches into a semi-circular amphitheatre rich with beech, sycamore and birch. The far end of a similar tunnel at Acharn, near Kenmore, opens onto a spectacular viewpoint overlooking the Falls of Acharn. The third Earl of Breadalbane had cut a winding T-plan tunnel into the hillside leading to this viewing pavilion. 'The approach to it is through a dark cavern in a thick wood, and it is built to command the full view of a vast cataract of 240 feet, almost perpendicular, surrounded on all sides, and crowned as high as the eye can reach, with wood'.[115] Dorothy Wordsworth visited it in 1803: 'Our guide opened a door, and we entered a dungeon-like passage, and, after walking some yards in total darkness found ourselves in a quaint appartment stuck over with moss, hung about with stuffed foxes and other wild animals, and ornamented with a library of wooden books covered with old leather backs, and mock furniture of a hermit's cell. At the end of the room, through a large bow window, we saw the waterfall . . . a very beautiful prospect'.[116]

It is quite probable that it was in response to visiting this viewpoint that Robert Burns had written the following poem in pencil over the chimney piece in the parlour of The Inn at Kenmore (by Taymouth) in 1787:

Poetic ardours in my bosom swell,
Lone wand'ring by the hermit's mossy cell;
The sweeping theatre of hanging woods,
The incessant roar of headlong tumbling floods

A growing fashion for using shells as part of the palette of grottos is exemplified by that at Newhailes, Musselburgh, and another one built in the same year at Gosford. The latter is decorated with ammonite shells. Shell patterns spread from the grotto to garden walls as at Cockenzie, whose pavilion has niches lined with sea shells. The word 'Hecla', picked out in tufa on the front of the pavilion, is thought to refer to the Icelandic volcano which erupted in 1783.

Grottos at the end of the nineteenth century were generally enhanced by the reuse of pieces of genuine antiquity: thus architec-

tural fragments from Dunblane Cathedral in the garden grotto at Oatfield House, and to complete the "antique" bathing house at Keir.

Moss houses, bowers, summer houses and hermitages formed part of the rustic family. The Scottish hermitage was more a rustic pavilion for viewing waterfalls than the monk-inhabited grotto favoured in England. It was a building from which to observe rather than being part of the experience itself; and the earliest may have

149

been that built at Corra Linn in 1708 by Sir James Carmichael of Bonnington, for the enjoyment of the Falls of Clyde. Before the construction of the hydro-electric station, this waterfall was one of the most dramatic in Britain, as we can still witness twice a year when the Electricity Board lets it go. The whole body of that river dashes over 'a vast precipice of craggy rocks, and covers the whole chasm with foam by the impetuosity of the torrent'. Carmichael installed a mirror in the back wall of the hermitage for the benefit of those 'who might suffer vertigo if looking directly at the Falls'; they could do so vicariously instead. It was visited by Thomas Pennant in 1772: 'The cataract is full in view, seen over the tops of trees and bushes, precipitating itself for an amazing way, from rock to rock, with short interruptions, forming a rude slope of furious foam. The sides are bounded by vast rocks, closed on their tops with trees; and on the summit and very verge of one is a ruined tower'.[117] By 1778 the hermitage had become ruinous.

A much better viewing pavilion is that overlooking the waterfall of the River Braan from its perch above a dramatic gorge at Dunkeld. Built by the second Duke of Atholl in 1758, it was set at first in a barren landscape, a garden of exotic trees subsequently planted around it. In 1783, the interior was transmogrified by George Steuart into 'Ossian's Hall'. The story is taken up by Dorothy Wordsworth: 'We were conducted into a small apartment, where the gardener desired us to look at a painting of the figure of Ossian, which, while he was telling us a story of the young artist who performed the work, disappeared, parting in the middle, flying assunder as if by the touch of magic and lo! we are at the entrance of a splendid room, which was almost dizzy and alive with waterfalls, that tumbled in all directions, the great cascade, which was opposite to the window that faced us being reflected in innumerable mirrors upon the ceiling and against the walls. We both laughed heartily which, no doubt, the gardener considered as high commendation'.[118] Her brother William apostrophised the scene:

> A gay saloon with waters dancing
> Upon the sight wherever glancing;
> One loud cascade in front, and lo!

> A thousand like it white as snow—
> Streams on the walls, and torrents foam.[119]

The rather less frivolous William Gilpin who had visited the place a number of years before, had been 'dismayed' by the use of coloured glass in the windows which he considered produced a bizarre effect; and Henry Skrine who visited it in 1796 on one of his three tours of Scotland, regarded it as 'whimsical and not without some effect; but the fitting up of the room with gilding and a great variety of looking glasses is insufferably tawdry'.[120] After being vandalised in 1812 and in 1869, it was acquired by the National Trust for Scotland in 1952 and, although drastically simplified, survives and is open to the public.

The Hermitage built at Dunkeld is not to be confused with the viewing platform; for it was described in 1762 as an 'enchantingly beautiful Retirement, fit for Contemplation and Study', something Ossian's Hall could never have been. The Hermitage was a two-storey structure, the lower being a cellar cut into rock and reached by a hatch through the floor. Bishop Forbes enjoyed his visit in 1771: 'The walls of the Hermitage are decorated with some very pretty prints . . . framed in Shell Work and with pieces of Roots of Trees having the natural Moss upon them, which greatly resemble different species of Rocks. There was one Frame of Shell Work peculiarly Curious, being the several kinds of Butterflies pasted on Paper by the Belly with the Wings expanded'.[121] The windows of this hexagonal pavilion could be thrown open to reveal nearby cascades, and waterworks played in the grotto below.

Moss Houses

On her visit to Bonnington Linn on the Clyde, in 1803, Dorothy Wordsworth was also taken to a Moss House: 'We came to a pleasure house called The Fog House, because it was lined with fog (moss). On the outside it resembled some of the huts in the prints belonging to Captain Cook's voyages; and within was like a haystack scooped out. It was circular, with a dome-like roof, a seat all round fixed to the wall, and a table in the middle, – seat, wall, roof and table all covered with moss in the neatest manner possible. It was

151

Interior of one of the rustic summerhouses at Drumlanrig showing patterning in brown and white moss on ceiling and walls above seating of intricately patterned larch rods.

snug as a bird's nest. We afterwards found that huts of the same kind were common in the pleasure grounds of Scotland, but we never saw any that were as beautifully wrought as this'.[122] Legend has it that it was in the circular, thatched Fog House at Ballochmyle, a funny little building with knobbly trees as columns, that Robert Burns first met his 'Bonnie Lass'.

Rustic summerhouses, occasionally built around the bole of a living tree (and in one case scooped from the trunk of a dead one) would have a plain pitched roof of reeds, heather or thatch; a larch-wood portico (thought to be in sympathy with the primitive form of the Doric order); sheltering walls of larch posts infilled with boards, rubble or thatch and fenestrated with arched or triangular windows. Walls and ceilings would be decorated with patterns of pine cones, chalk or coal dust stencils, and figures in crests formed from coloured and white moss. It is not surprising that buildings constructed of such perishable materials rarely survive. However, the rustic summerhouse at Kinnaird Castle, near Perth, built by Lady Carnegie in 1800, has a pine cone ceiling, cobbled floor, and lattice windows. A similar, dated 1834, may be found beside the

croquet lawn at Traquair. The most impressive collection, however, is at Drumlanrig whose buildings feature the entire palette. It is possible there to discern the influence of Charles McIntosh. The 1845, Bavarian summer house at Brodick Castle is only one of three to survive, its interior lavishly finished with a ceiling festooned in different patterns of cones and larch work, apparently executed by Bavarian craftsmen. The boarded timber walls are encrusted with artificial creepers, so that the whole structure appears to grow organically from the ground. Similar techniques of rustic larch work and pattern panels are employed at the canopy garden seat at Newton Don, by Kelso, which has the appearance of a rustic Turkish tent.[123]

Brodick Castle's Bavarian summerhouse ceiling is festooned in arrangements of different sorts of pine cones and larch rods, some stained green. (Courtesy of the National Trust for Scotland.)

153

Rustic garden seat at Newton Don. (Royal Commission on Ancient Monuments, Scotland.)

The picturesque primitiveness implied by the rustic craze broadened to encompass functional buildings such as cottages, gardener's houses, and in some cases farm buildings and the Mains itself. It was little more than an appropriately rustic dress for practical houses for estate workers – architecture's answer, if you like, to Laura Ashley. A good example is the little, harled and thatched

154

cottage, fenced with its own knot garden at Mellerstain. Restored in 1978, it has lost some of its elaborate details, but the fireplace and the rustic larch work table survive yet.

Skyline-fillers

Structures on the tops of hills were designed either to be seen from the house or within the estate (and therefore private); or to broadcast to the world at large.

The Repentance Tower at Hoddom is one of the earliest. Built in 1560 in expiation of the betrayal and resultant murder of twelve hostages, it was erected by the perpetrator John Maxwell, and inscribed with the single word 'Repentance'. It inspired further poesy, in this case a ballad by Kirkpatrick Sharpe, whose middle verse runs thus:

> Repentance! The signal of my bale
> Built of lasting stane
> Ye lang shall tell the bluidy tale
> When I am dead and gane.

It is possibly Scotland's only tower of atonement.

Prospect Towers were created to take advantage of the view; and commemorative towers were constructed to celebrate military success or dynastic change. Romantic towers and follies were built to enhance the natural glories of the hillside, gorge, cliff or landscape; and many were really built as a subtle means of providing employment at times of slump, while at the same time deriving publicity and goodwill. It is arguable that the Scottish landowner had less need of new artificial ruins than his English counterpart; after all, he had so much of the real article readily available. Once families had quit their ancestral tower, it usually remained neglected and crumbling until a new generation perceived its picturesque potential. Thereafter, it grew in importance as part of the estate's impedimenta. The 1550 Peel Tower at Castle Semple, by Lochwinnoch, became an island playground. The seventeenth century Staneyhill Tower at Hopetoun was transformed to a hilltop shelter for the occupants of the south deer park, while the towers of Bailzieland, Logan and Monimail were all enfolded into garden walls as picturesque objects. Cadzow Castle, the fifteenth century seat of the Hamilton Family, was reduced to the status of a picturesque folly; a cliffside underground passage along the very cliff of the steep Avon Gorge, within the ruins, providing the necessary thrill.

Few examples of the purely self-indulgent ruin or folly survive in Scotland. The Gate of Negrapatam, built on Fyrish Hill above Novar House near Invergordon by General Sir Hector Monroe, commemorated his successful capture of that gate from the Dutch forces in India in 1781. Nine large rubble columns form arches at the centre, visible for miles around. Its accuracy to the original was doubted by Robert Southey: 'There are some odd edifices on the summits, which he is said to have designed as imitations of the hillforts in India'. The Malakof Arch at Murthly was a hilltop Arc-de-Triomphe of colossal proportions, blown up after the Second World War.

Generally, those paying for skyline structures wanted more out of them. Some two-dimensional castellated structures were erected in the manner of stage sets to close vistas, like the Fort erected on rising ground above Taymouth Castle. Attributed to John Baxter and probably built in 1760–1774, the Fort consists of crenellated screen walls linked to two round pavilions, each originally topped with a domed roof surmounted by an inverted Turkish sickle.[124] 'Some small field and garrison pieces, which are fired on special occasions'[125] were added in 1800. In 1761, the Duke of Atholl decided to build one of his own at Blair, "The Whim" and ordered 'A moddle to be made of a Wall with Battlements and five arched windows to be built on the Top of Den Hill. The Wall to be 110 ft long, and 22 ft, to the Top of the Battlements'.[126]

Prospect Towers

Mock castellations, Gothick fantasy or indeed any design that was calculated to inspire sensations of romance and antiquity proved popular for the Prospect or Outlook Towers which sprouted on hill tops predominantly between 1740 and 1850. Their function was to provide hilltop shelter, not unlike remote summer houses. At the

very least, there would be a simple tower with steps, offering the prospect of a grand outlook over the policies.

William Adam is credited with the 1741 design of such a tower at the Drum, which not only closed the vista but provided a view-point over the deer park. An octagonal pavilion on the top of Kenmuir Hill was built by Captain William McDowall in the 1770s so that he could gaze down upon his deer park at Castle Semple. Most people visiting Inveraray are teased by what seems to be an ancient tower at the summit of Duniquaich, frowning down upon the castle and town. That was the effect intended by John Adam and Roger Morris who designed the forty-five foot high two-storey tower to be literally, the, high point of the tour round the Inveraray policies in 1745. Not that visitors were expected to exert them-selves: they would be carried up to this pavilion in the sky in horse and carriage. It offers stupendous views down Loch Fyne, over the estate and the River Aray some 250 metres below.[127] Barely a generation later, visitors were convinced of its ancient origins. Lady

'The Whim' at Blair is a two-dimensional screen flanked by twin openwork pavilions, forming a vista from the castle.

157

Temple of Venus crowning Doune Hill above Duff House. The statue of Venus has departed.

Margaret's Tower, erected by Lady Campbell at Lochnell, by Benderloch in 1754, is a structure of Vanbruggian massing. Castellated, with angle turrets, semi-circular arches, and a turnpike stair lit by lunettes, it leads to a viewing platform offering some of the finest views in Scotland over Loch Linnhe, Loch Etive and the Sound of Mull. On special occasions like the Laird's birthday, it was lit up as a beacon. The hexagonal Baron's Folly at Monteviot, atop the yellow ragwort-covered summit, offers a fabulous panorama over Borders countryside to the deep varied blues and greens of the distant Cheviot Hills. John Paterson's Gothick Tower at Fasque is a composition with a central pavilion linked to twin hexagonal towers, pointed windows and *quatrefoil* decoration.

A number of Prospect Towers were designed for the stimulation of awe, probably happiest seen above a chasm at midnight with a full moon and owls. Typically, internal stairs would lead to a viewing platform enclosed by a crenellated parapet, and the base would sometimes be provided with screen walls to maximise the dramatic qualities of a hilltop site. Robert Adam's sketchbooks contain a variety of proposals along these lines, and smaller versions continued to be built well into the nineteenth century. The Gothick octagonal viewing tower at Gartencaber, near Thornhill, was erected by William Murdoch (just before he scandalised his neighbours by marrying his housekeeper) for the simple enjoyment of the 'wide and beautiful view it commands on both sides'. Anybody, upon making proper application, could have access to ascend on its unique external cantilevered staircase. The sadly derelict Smith's Folly at Craigend, by Milngavie, was altogether a more highly crafted object: octagonal, two storeys in fine stonework, with Gothick windows, vaulting and *trefoil* decoration. The visitors mounting the spiral masonry staircase would emerge through a vaulted, bossed ceiling into a roof-level belvedere, overlooking the Mugdock Castle policies, which commanded the frontier between the Highlands to the north, and the Lowlands of the Clyde plain to the south. Influenced by the picturesque appearance of the castles which line the cliffs along the River Rhine, the ninth Earl of Kinnoul constructed Kinnoul and Binhill Towers sometime after 1813, on the edge of cliffs which drop 100 metres sheer to the Tay

Octagonal pavilion atop Kenmuir Hill overlooking Castle Semple and offering shelter today only for sheep.

158

below. A walk through adjacent woodland (best at twilight) leads to a grassy clearing on the top of a precipice, where one tower clasps determinedly to the crooked crag, and the silhouette of the other just breaks the skyline further along.

Prospect Towers of the later nineteenth century were rather less dramatic. The 1832 five-stage Reform Tower at Meet Hill House was a celebration of the great Reform Act, in the form of a viewing tower and observatory. Fitting-out was never completed. Reputedly, the brick-built octagonal observatory tower at Pitfour was built by Admiral Ferguson in 1845 to overlook a canal which he planned to have dug between his newly created lake and the sea some ten miles away. It is said that when the money ran out for that enterprise, the tower was used for watching deer-hunting and horse-racing on a course cut out of the forest. The early nineteenth century, three-storey harled brick lookout tower, protected by an evergreen hedge and a ha-ha on the top of Cormie Hill at Raith Park, in Fife, is possibly the largest in girth, approximately eight metres square. For many years it was used as a private museum.

Commemorative memorial towers and obelisks were a gauge of either the patriotism or the self-esteem of the landowner: the more remote the site and difficult the construction, the greater the satisfaction derived. Generally, the landowner paid. Penielheugh, a fifty metre high structure designed by Archibald Elliot in 1815, crowns a hill at Monteviot. Two hundred and twenty-eight steps are required to take the visitor to the top. A lead plaque proclaims: 'To the Duke of Wellington and the British Army William Kerr Marquis of Lothian and his Tenantry, dedicate this monument XXX June MDCCCXV'. The 1806, octagonal Nelson Tower near Forres commemorates Trafalgar with a viewing point over the Moray Firth, whereas the round, crenellated tower on the hillside above the House of the Binns, near Linlithgow, commemorates Waterloo. It was built in 1826 as the result of a wager by Sir James Dalyell. There are two towers on the Panmure Estate. The first inscribed to 'James, Earl of Panmure and Countess Margaret', displays their marriage stone of 1694. The second is a gigantic, round, buttressed tower of red sandstone added in 1839 to a design by John Henderson, called the Panmure Testimonial.

The brick observatory in the woods at Pitfour is a tower within a tower. At the top, the viewing gallery was used to watch horse racing.

Prospect tower at Gartincaber with an unusual external cantilevered stair. Both internal rooms had fireplaces.

159

Nelson's Tower, Forres, built 1806, provides a viewpoint over the Moray Firth. (Royal Commission on Ancient Monuments, Scotland.)

An obelisk has a memorial purpose, and usually takes the form of a square stone shaft tapering to a pyramid at the top. Even without a memorial purpose, and it is uncertain whether the Balvenie Pillar which crowns Tom-na-Croiche at Blair had such a purpose, the obelisk still symbolised the hand of civilised man. Erected in 1755, the Pillar was designed with a gilded ball on top and a lean-to shelter around the base.

The obelisk in Cauldshoulders Park, Penicuik, was erected in 1759 by Sir James Clerk in memory of the poet Allan Ramsay. Its top takes the unusual form of being pierced with oculi (or holes) and an archway at the base shelters inscriptions praising the poet. An equally fine obelisk at Haddo reveres the memory of the brother of the Fourth Earl of Aberdeen who was killed at Waterloo in 1815. The prominent 1856 obelisk at Tyninghame is in memory of 'Thomas Sixth Earl of Haddington, born 1680 died in 1735, who at a period of the greatest national depression, had the foresight and energy to set the example of planting on an extensive scale, and to be an active and successful promoter of agricultural improvement'. A reproduction of the thirteenth century Queen Eleanor's Cross[128] was designed by William Atkinson at Taymouth in 1831, in memory

160

of Mary, Countess of Breadalbane. The cross is set in a nine-step base, with a stone door leading to a mid-stage staircase. A poignant memorial paid for 'by the people of Dunrobin' commemorates Harriet, Duchess of Sutherland, and the foundation stone was laid by Queen Victoria in 1872. Below its elaborate Victorian decoration, there is the inscription 'Neither failing sight nor altered health will make dear Dunrobin less vivid, nor change the love I bear to Sutherland'.

The MacGregor Memorial, hidden within the trees at Lanrick Castle has perhaps the most curious history. It symbolises the return to normality of the MacGregor Clan, or Clan Albyn who, until the late eighteenth century, had been forbidden to use their name upon pain of death. The proscription dated from an Act of the Privy Council in 1613. Instead, they had adopted the names of other clans such as Drummond, Murray and Campbell. The memorial was probably erected by Sir Euan Murray MacGregor in the early nineteenth century, at the time when Lanrick had become known for a short while as Clan Gregor Castle. It takes the form of a stone tree-trunk, but it has been said that there is a real tree-trunk enclosed within, upon which three columns rise to support a platform which bears a further column reaching up to the sky.

Victorian sentimentality led to a number of monuments recording the passing of favourite pets and animals. The sculpture of a horse called King Tom by Ernest Boehm, 1873, was brought to Dalmeny House near Edinburgh from Mentmore in Buckinghamshire. A statue at Hoddom commemorates a favourite otterhound which died of pneumonia in 1898 after overlong immersion in the river. Drumlanrig has a good pet cemetery with little headstones to the estate's dogs and cats, and statues commemorating Queen Victoria's favourite dogs may be found at Balmoral.

The memorials on the hilltops surrounding Balmoral are, however, of a different order. A brisk uphill walk, through conifers redolent of warm resin and sweet broom, leads one to a viewpoint with large cairns recording marriages and deaths within Queen Victoria's own family. The largest cairn, some ten metres high, is to the memory of 'Albert, the Great and Good . . . raised by his heart-broken widow Victoria R August 21st 1862'.

At House of the Binns, Midhope Tower built 1826 commemorates Trafalgar.

Memorials and Mausolea

Memorial column at Aberlour erected circa 1834, subsequently collapsed, and was rebuilt in 1888, with a unicorn replacing the original granite ball finial. (RCAHMS)

The obelisk at Haddo is dedicated to the memory of the Fourth Earl of Aberdeen's brother.

One intriguing result of enclosure was that several churches and chapels, particularly the fine collegiate churches built in the period 1400–1560 which had served the original communities adjacent to the towers, now found themselves isolated within country house policies. Their congregations were exiled beyond the walls outside, usually provided with a new church. Some of the old buildings were neglected and vanished, and some turned into romantic follies. Superb dog-tooth chancel arches of the twelfth century St Baldred's Chapel grace the garden at Tyninghame, after the fine stonework of its walls had been removed to build the nearby stable block. The majority of such buildings were reused as family burial vaults, churches or mausolea. In 1753, the fifteenth century collegiate church of St Cuthbert, at Yester, was given an early Rococo Gothick frontage, and thus renewed, remained as the family burial place once the new parish church in Gifford had been completed. Alternatively landed families colonised aisles in the local parish church which, when the original was rebuilt, as frequently occurred in the nineteenth century, are often all that remains of the older buildings.

Free-standing estate mausolea did not emerge as a Scottish building type until the late eighteenth century, and thereafter took two forms; simple unostentatious structures placed on raised ground, much in the form of medieval chapels, or grandiose architectural monuments. Few contained a chapel that was used on any regular basis.

Mausolea of the simpler sort worth a visit, include those of the Massy-Beresfords on Macbiehill built in 1769; to Campbell of Barbreck built in 1795, for the family of Macquarrie at Gruline, Mull built in 1874, and to Maclaine of Luchbuy, also in Mull, in 1871. Continuing numbers of small mid-nineteenth century memorial chapels were constructed, usually with a steeply pitched roof, above ornament including a small rose window, and some small revivalist Celtic crosses.

Since a family mausoleum implied either a long lineage (an essential social asset) or could assist in the creation of one, some families aspired to much greater. Sir John Sinclair of Ulbster[129] erected

162

Harald's Tower on the rising ground overlooking Thurso Bay in 1790, putatively intending to commemorate Harald, a former Jarl of Caithness, who is believed to have been killed near the site in 1196. However, it was clear that Sinclair was claiming him for an ancestor, for the plaque records 'The burial place of the Sinclairs of Ulbster'. The mausoleum is crude, in imitation of antiquity, comprising a circle with blunt, pinnacle pencil turrets rising at intervals. Sinclair himself is thought to be buried at the other mausoleum of the Sinclairs of Ulbster, a four-square building set within enclosing walls that once demarcated the graveyard of old St Martin's Chapel.[130] At about the same time, on the site of a Carmellite chapel, James Duff the second Earl of Fife constructed an elaborate new mausoleum in the policies of Duff House by Banff, in which he reinterred his father. He added a range of putative ancestors and, ignoring as inconvenient his own lineage of the Duffs of Keithmore (farmers near Dufftown), he purloined the tombs of genuinely ancient Duffs of Muldavit from Cullen Kirk (dates altered to increase their antiquity), and a fine seventeenth century tomb from the ruins of St Mary's Church in Banff. The building is in the plasterwork-Gothick antique style, with sprocketed finials extending above an eaves' course of roundels.

Mausolea began to dominate the landscape. In 1795, Robert Mitchell designed an octagonal mausoleum on a knoll, in the form of a temple with eight thin columns, at Preston Hall. He described its purpose thus: 'The prospect from the North Front is through a noble avenue, which terminates with a mausoleum erected by Sir John Callander in memory of his later brother Alexander Callander Crighton. In the chapel of this building, there is intended to be placed a monument of marble, as executed of appropriate design'.[131] The marble monument has not yet been installed, the memorial plaque remains uninscribed, and the vault empty. The large ashlar pyramid at Gosford, designed to house the remains of the seventh Earl in 1794/5, has a columned portico against each of its four sides. Gates to the encircling wall have piers marked 'Exploratur', which are surmounted by crouching lead figures with scythes or flaying knives, apparently copies from the statue of the Flayer of Marsyas at the Uffizzi Gallery, Florence. The mausoleum at Mellerstain is

The Balvenie Pillar at Tom-na-Croiche, Blair, was erected in 1755.

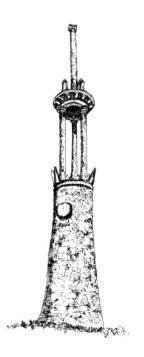

Lanrick 'Tree', a curious structure which stands hidden amongst trees, celebrates the history of the MacGregor Clan.

163

Remains of St Baldred's Chapel, a twelfth century structure partially demolished to provide stone for the nearby stable block at Tyninghame.

situated at the end of a cross walk called The Grove. It takes the form of a temple, and the frontage is inscribed with the following verses:

> The pious parents rear'd this hallowed Place
> A Monument for them and for their race
> Descendants make it your successive cares
> That no Degenerate Dust e'er mix with Theirs
> Built by George Baillie of Jerviswoode Esq
> and Lady Grisell Baillie AD 1736

The fifth Earl of Dunmore was probably responsible for the conversion of the barrel-vaulted ground floor of ruinous fifteenth century Elphinstone Tower as a family burial vault in 1802. In 1807, the Earl of Mansfield commissioned William Atkinson to remodel the 1748 family mausoleum set high on the artificial hill of Tom-a-Mhoid (Gaelic for Moot Hill) at Scone. It was transformed into a style in keeping with the new Scone Palace, and is decorated with four corner towers with sprocketed finials.

The heroic and monumental qualities of early nineteenth century

164

The pyramidal family mausoleum at Gosford.

neoclassicism proved ideal for mausolea. One of the finest examples is that at Callendar House, Falkirk, commissioned by the widow of William Forbes, whose drum towers above the surrounding trees. The design by Archibald Elliot is a Greek Doric temple comprising twelve columns set upon a heavily rusticated podium. Above the main entrance is the couplet from Lucian carved in Greek: 'Mortals' possessions are mortal, and all things us pass by; if not, at any rate we pass them by'.

About 1843, dissastisfied with the state of the family tomb in the Church at Hamilton, the tenth Duke of Hamilton sought to achieve something more imposing in line with his nickname 'El Magnifico'. The result, designed by David Bryce, is a truly gigantic, opulent rotunda, thirty-six metres in height. There is an overwhelming sense of power which stems from the huge pieces of masonry used in its construction, and from the massive cast-bronze doors modelled on Ghiberti's entry to the Baptistry in Florence. The floor within is inlaid with green porphyry, pink Peterhead granite, jasper and several different marbles. Symbolic carvings by Handyside Ritchie represent life, death, and immortality. Yet although the Duke was finally laid to rest here in an ancient Egyptian sarcophagus of finely

Late eighteenth century proposal at Callendar for a memorial tower.

165

Just above the Waterfall Pool at Kelburn stands the Monument, designed in 1775 by Robert Adam and commissioned by the Third Countess of Glasgow in memory of her husband.

The mausoleum at Monteviot, on high ground which looks across to other estate structures: Baron's Folly and Penielheugh.

carved green basalt, the interior was never fully completed. It transpired to have the longest reverberation time in Europe, lasting some fifteen seconds, thus acoustically impossible to use for a service. Subsidence from coal-mining caused structural damage, as it caused the collapse of the Palace nearby. Bodies of the Duke and his ancestors had to be moved elsewhere in 1921. In 1975, owner-ship passed to Strathclyde Regional Council, and the mausoleum is now stabilised, repaired, and open from time to time to the public. El Magnifico's son, the eleventh Duke, was more modest in his aspirations. He is laid to rest in a relatively unpretentious rotunda by Charles Wilson, elsewhere on the estate. His 1869 bust by Mossman is preserved in the courtyard at Chatelherault.

There remained in the Monteviot estate the challenge of an uncrowned hilltop (the other summits being occupied already by Penielheugh and Baron's Folly). It is now the setting for a Victorian neo-Roman pavilion flanked by two stone lions, which com-memorates Sir Thomas Monteith. Wooden entry doors, studded with iron rosettes, swing open to reveal a tomb flanked by carved angels. The chamber is dark and enormously high, its domed vault

The Forbes mausoleum at Callendar, built in 1816.

lit by four concentric rings of six-pointed stars. Originally those stars were glazed: the wind now whistles and moans eerily through.

Sir George Bullough, considering the family tomb on the island of Rhum should be improved, dynamited his father's mausoleum. Visitors will come across the result in a curious way. From the relative shelter of Kinloch Castle at the head of Loch Scresort, a wild rough track winds up into the hills across the island amid stark scenery. Hilltops with Viking names rise above glens grazed by free-roaming, long-horned, woolly orange Highland cattle. Where the track runs down to overlook the sea, in a singularly remote and beautiful setting, may be found Sir George Bullough's own desolate mausoleum: a forceful classical temple of dark red sandstone sheltering three granite burial casks. Few places could better exemplify the notion of *memento mori*, and on a fine day, it would be hard to imagine a more peaceful spot. Fragments of dressed stone and bright polychromatic Victorian tiling shine through a hole on the ground less than fifty metres distant. These are the remains of the dynamited barrel-vault of the former terracotta-faced burial chapel erected by John Bullough. His crest is still visible.

Sailing Into the Sunset

Buildings on Scottish estates are so diverse that it has been difficult to categorise or group them. As soon as a type appears, a landowner or architect will appear to confound it. Some buildings simply will not fit easily into the category of food buildings, pavilions, or structures in the landscape – sometimes because they combined all of them. So this book ends with the humble boathouse: something to look from, something to look at, something in which to relax, and something to emphasise the owner's prescience.

It is tempting to think of the ornamental boathouse as an exclusively Victorian phenomenon, but they were clearly built much earlier. One was built at Loch Dhu at Inveraray in 1752, and the 1790 boathouse at Gosford survives yet (although it lacks a lead statue of Perseus which originally surmounted its arched front). It is flanked by buttresses each topped with a sphinx. The boathouse at Ardmaddy, Argyll, was carved from the living rock and may, as at Culzean, have been used to shelter a lifeboat manned by estate

168

ELEVATION LOOKING TO LAKE

SIDE ELEVATION

Grandiose proposal for a boathouse from John Starforth's book 'Architecture of the Park' published in Edinburgh in 1890. (Royal Commission on Ancient Monuments, Scotland.)

workers. Four pairs of timber columns supported a trussed roof, and it is fronted by a 1795 Gothick screen wall.[132]

Boathouses are ornamental shelters for boats. That at Penicuik was finished with whale jaw-bones and heather thatch, whereas the pinnacled boat shelter at Fyvie Castle, built in 1816, is dominated by a sailing ship's figurehead. Little now remains of the rubble, Gothick-arched boat house at Pitfour, possibly built in 1830; indeed it is possible that it was designed as a purpose-built ruin. In the later nineteenth century, boathouses became equipped with an upstairs saloon and at least one balcony, as a matter of course. More elaborate ones incorporated retiring rooms and a landing stage. The

1864 boathouse at Dochfour is a good illustration. Deep eaves shelter a balcony supported upon ornamental iron brackets. External stairs lead to an upstairs chamber. To judge by the boathouse at Dougarie, built in 1890 by J. J. Burnet, boathouses of a later generation were even more opulent yet: for it presents an unusual twin-gabled design with widely swept eaves and a long slipway. Within, the walls are studded with curios and hunting trophies, and a series of cartoons drawn directly onto the plaster by Prosperi, depict visitors to the estate. There are two, equally fine, mid-nineteenth century boathouses at Loch Inch, by Castle Kennedy.

John Starforth's *Architecture of the Park* depicted boathouses as elaborate architectural monuments with generous accommodation, but few appear to have been built in Scotland. There is a grandiose example at Manderston, dated 1894, and at Mount Melville (now Craigtoun Park, near St Andrews), Paul Waterhouse designed a ponderous boathouse for the Younger family. It had circular windows, and an enormous mannered keystone set into a generous round-arched opening. Dwarf walls along the waterside linked it to a curious collection of garden pavilions. All have now gone. Possibly the last gasp of the building type is below the immense towers guarding the eastern entrance to Dunecht (see p 87) which, in addition to acting as lodges, shelter a fine granite boathouse on the shore of Loch of Skene.

Chapter 6

Twentieth Century Postscript

Yester. Glazed summerhouse fashioned from an old station clocktower.

Free-standing garden pavilions of the latter part of the twentieth century have been distinguished by a general lack of whimsy, imagination and elegance. Investment in estates, once represented by monuments, obelisks, mausolea, and temples, have been replaced by investment in agribusiness. Modern technology has rendered the doocot, icehouse, fish pond, game larder and dairy redundant. Our changing culture no longer values vistas, commissions chapels, nor magnifies mausolea.

There have been some recent signs of change. A treillage pavilion has been reconstructed, and a new Gothick summer house built in the gardens of Tyninghame. The clock-tower from the old Caledonian Station, Edinburgh, has been re-erected at Yester as a glazed summer house. The cupola designed by Charles Rennie Mackintosh for the top of Pettigrew's store in Glasgow has been repaired and used as a summer house for the Environment Show Pavilion in the Glasgow Garden Festival. A water garden has been laid out as a relief map of Scotland at the Black Barony Hotel near Peebles, and a nearby eighteenth century garden temple has been restored.

Among the more unusual touches of the new generation must be the Moon-Viewing Pavilion, a kind of pyramid surmounted by an arch, which rises from the garden within the enclosing walls which surround the old tower of Kinkell. The achievement by Ian Hamilton Finlay and Andrew Townsend at Little Sparta, with a garden, Wilderness, sundials, and, set into the side of a hill a domed grotto (dedicated to Dido and Aeneas who consummated their love in a cave while sheltering from a thunderstorm), indicates that there is hope yet.

People have more leisure than ever before. There is a growing taste for the unusual, the bizarre, the remote and the neglected. The Friends of the Earth, or the Greens might well find a re-examination

171

Charles Rennie Mackintosh designed cupola from Pettigrew's store, Glasgow, on view at the 1988 Glasgow Garden Festival.

of these low technology buildings useful. They represent the achievement of large communities of people who fed and sustained themselves without reliance upon artificial sources of energy or fertiliser.

This book has attempted to introduce to the reader why such structures were built, who built them, and where to find them; and above all to convey the sheer pleasure of success in that endeavour.

172

Notes

CHAPTER 1

1. 'The National Trust for Scotland Guide - A Complete Introduction to the Buildings, Gardens, Coast and Country Owned by the National Trust for Scotland.' Compiled and Edited by Robin Prentice. Jonathan Cape 3rd Edition 1981 p.36.

2. Kinross: 'The house is a picture, 'tis all beauty; the stone is white and fine, the order regular, the contrivance excellent; the workmanship exquisite . . .'. Daniel Defoe; 'A Tour Through The Whole Island of Great Britain' (1724-6). Edited by Pat Rogers. Penguin English Library repr. 1979. Book 13 p.630.

3. Bruce seems to have been held in high regard by his contemporaries; Sir John Clerk called him 'the chief introducer of Architecture in this country' and Daniel Defoe called him the 'Kit Wren of Scotland'.

4. Captain John Slezer may have come over from Holland, and the first references to him are in 1690. 'Theatrum Scotiae', a collection of some 60 drawings – many being bird's eye views of country houses – was first published in 1693 though it may have been begun as early as 1672.

5. Illustrated by a map of Alloa engraved by L. Sturt 1710 from a survey by Bernard Lens see SRO RHP 13258 No 2.

6. John Macky: 'A Journey Through Scotland in Familiar Letters From a Gentleman Here, to his Friends Abroad'. 3rd Volume, 2nd Edition. London MDCCXXIX Letter 10 Stirling p.178.

7. Ibid. Letter 4 Edinburgh. p.64.

8. William Mackintosh of Borlum: 'An Essay on Ways and Means for Inclosing, Fallowing, Planting etc, Scotland; and that in 16 years at farthest, by a lover of his country Edinburgh 1729. p.23. (Mackintosh, 1662–1743, was a Brigadier in the 1715 Uprising, and was imprisoned for many years in Edinburgh Castle).

9. 'Boswell's Journal of a Tour to the Hebrides with Samuel Johnson LLD' with notes by Scott, Croker, Chambers and Others. 2 Volumes, Constable and Co. 1898. (First Published London 1785) Vol 1, p.70.

10. Ibid Vol 1 p.187.

11. Defoe op. cit. Book 11 p.567.

12. Sir John Clerk of Penicuik: Publications of the Scottish History Society Volume XIII 'Clerk of Penicuik's Memoirs (extracted by himself from his own Journals 1676–1755)' edited by John M. Gray Edinburgh 1892 (1738) p.182.

13. John Macky op. cit. p.149 letter 9 Dumferling.

14. Ibid p.31 letter 3 Inverask.

15. William Mackintosh of Borlum op. cit. quoting. Act Primo Georgii Regis p.318.

16. Ibid p.XXV

17. The period 1750–1800 was rich in the construction of estate villages in Scotland – some 150 were built, concentrated in the more fertile areas such as Lothian and Aberdeenshire, funded by rich officials returning from service abroad and from rapid growth in the industries of cotton, flax and wool. James Boswell visited Laurencekirk in 1773 and reported: 'Lord Gardenstoun is the proprietor . . . and has encouraged the building of a manufacturing village, of which he is exceedingly fond, and has written a pamphlet on it, as if he had founded Thebes.'

18. An early publication setting out methods for improving lands by such means was James Donaldsons 'Husbandry Anatomized' Published 1697.

REFERENCES;

NMRS
National Monuments
Record (Scotland)
RHP
Register House Plan
SDD
Scottish Development
Department
SRO
Scottish Record Office

173

19. William Mackintosh of Borlum *op. cit.* p.155. It was suggested that 'English day labourers' should be imported 'from the counties excelling in good Hedges and fine plowing' namely Devon and Hertfordshire.

20. Robert Maxwell: *'Select Transactions of the Honourable The Society of Improvers in the Knowledge of Agriculture in Scotland'*, Edinburgh, 1743 p.vi.

21. John Smith *'Oriental Style Garden Structures in Middle 18th Century Scotland'* Unpublished thesis presented to the RIAS for the Thomas Ross Prize, Edinburgh 1987 quoting BCR Box 42.11(1)9.

22. Roy's maps c1750 of Haddington show clearly the contrast between the broad open rigs of the old system and the clearly geometric organisation into rectangles of the enclosed farms.

23. Batty Langley: *'New Principles of Gardening or the Laying Out and Planting of Parterres, Groves, Wildernesses, Labyrinths, Avenues, Parks etc. after a more Grand and Rural Manner than has been done before'* London MDCCXXVIII p.XI.

24. Ibid 'What a shame it is, to destroy a noble oak of two or three hundred years growth, that always produces a pleasant shade and graceful prospect for the sake of making a trifling grass plot or flower knot regular'. p.X.

25. Sir John Clerk *op. cit.* p.239.

26. Thomas Pennant *'A Tour in Scotland and Voyage to the Hebrides.'* MDCCLXXII. Chester MDCCLXXIV. p.92.

27. J. C. Loudon 1812 *'Observations on Laying Out Farms In The Scotch Style, adapted to England'*.

28. Coade Stone was one of the most successful of these artificial stones. In fact it was a fired terracotta used in increasing quantities from about 1769 until the closure of the works in 1840. The 1784 catalogue lists some 800 items ranging from chimney pots to garden statuary.

29. Charles McIntosh: *'Book of the Garden'* 1853.

30. More detailed statistics, including a figure of 452 demolitions or ruins since 1900, can be seen in *'Lost Houses of Scotland'*, by Save Britains Heritage, published 1980.

CHAPTER 2

31. John Macky *op. cit.*; Letter 12 Glasgow. p.281.

32. Dorothy Wordsworth *'Recollections of a Tour Made in Scotland'*. Edited J. C. Shairp, 1803 repr 1894. Third edition p.46. In greater detail; 'The house stands very sweetly in complete retirement; it has its gardens and terraces one above another, with flights of steps between, box-trees and yew-trees cut in fantastic shapes, flower borders and summer-houses; and still below, apples and pears were hanging in abundance on the branches of large old trees, which grew intermingled with the natural wood, elms, beeches, etc., even to the waters edge. The whole place is in perfect harmony with the taste of our ancestors, and the yews and hollies are shaven as nicely, and the gravel walks and flower borders kept in as exact order, as if the spirit of the first architect of the terraces still presided over them.'

33. H. Inigo Triggs: *'Formal Gardens in England & Scotland'*. Batsford. See plate 78, for a bird's eye view of the proposals.

34. Sir Robert Lorimer quoted by Sir H. Maxwell in *'Scottish Gardens'*, London. 1911, p.169.

35. For drawings of the arrangement at Dalkeith see Charles MacIntosh: *'Book of the Garden'*. Lean-to's without windows were used for cultivation of mushrooms, rhubarb, seakale, chicory, hyacinth and lilly of the valley.

36. Ochterlony of Guynd: *'Registrum de Panmure'*, The Honourable Harry Maule of Kelly, 1733 reprinted 1874. Volume 1 p.CLXI. The carvings on the East side of the garden wall depict the Planetary Deities (Saturn, Jupiter, Mars, Sol or Sun, Venus, Mercury, Luna); on the South side the Liberal Arts (grammatica, rhetorica, dialectica, arithmetica, musica, geometria—the astronomy, panel has disappeared), and on the West side the Cardinal Virtues (fides, spes, iustitia, caritas, prudentia, fortitudo, temperantia). The initials IB on some of the carvings are taken to refer to Iorg Bentz, or Georg Pencz. Pedimented niches between the panels include recesses for bee holes and nesting birds.

37. A map of Edinburgh 1647 shows extensive knot gardens laid out all around Heriot's Hospital, and on the other side of Greyfriars Kirk almost down to Holyrood house.

38. The twin gazebos at Traquair House probably date from the late 17th century additions by James Smith; the south pavilion is the most complete, featuring a panelled interior and wooden ceiling boards with a painted roundel depicting 'The Toilet of Venus'.

39. *'Richard Pococke Bishop of Meath: Tours in Scotland 1747, 1750, 1760. From the original M.S. and drawings in the British Museum.'* Edited D. W. Kemp, reprinted Edinburgh 1887 by the Scottish History Society. p.230.

40. John Reid *'The Scots Gardiner'* 1683. This book was so well received it was reprinted well into the 18th Century, with a further reprint by Mainstream Publications in 1988.

41. William Cobbett *'The English Gardener'* London 1829 Chapter II paragraph 16.

42. For example, 120 tulip roots, sold at auction near Amsterdam in 1637, fetched £8437—according to Charles MacIntosh.

43. See SRO/GD/112/20/1/31/2.

44. See report *'An Inventory of Gardens and Designed Landscapes in Scotland'* by Land Use Consultants to The Countryside Commission for Scotland and the Historic Buildings and Monuments Directorate 1988 SDD. Chapter 2 p.98. Sir Herbert Maxwell noted these varieties of flowers from a tapestry made c1730 by the wife of the 3rd Baronet at Monreith, Dumfries and Galloway.

45. Thus refuting the much quoted, but utterly inaccurate view 'as for fruit, for their gransire Adams sake they never planted any, and for other trees, had Christ been betrayed in this country (as doubtable he should, had he come as a stranger), Judas had sooner found the Grace of Repentance, than a tree to hang himself on' attributed to Sir Anthony Weldon who accompanied King James VI back to Scotland in 1617.

46. Land Use Consultants *op. cit.* Chapter 4. p.345.

47. Ochterlony of Guynd: *op. cit.* p.LXVVII.

48. Ibid p.LXVII. Some 150 years later, Nicol in *'The Scotch Forcing Gardener'* 1797 recorded widespread growing of grapes in Scotland 'this delicious and justly esteemed fruit is now cultivated with such general eagerness in this country that a garden unprovided with one or more compartments for its production is not only reckoned incomplete, but hardly to be met with.'

49. Roger Gale 1739 from 'The Family Memories of the Rev. William Stukely' Surtees Society, 1882 quoted by *'Furor Hortensis: Essays on the History of the English Landscape Garden in Memory of H. F. Clarke'*, edited P. Willis Elysium Press 1974.

50. J. C. Loudon: *'Improvements in Hothouses'* 1805 yet only a few years later he was able to recommend a morning walk to the kitchen garden as 'delightful' in *'Hints on the Formation of Pleasure Grounds.'* 1812.

51. See SRO/GD112/20/1/31.

52. See SRO/GD20/1/31/7.

53. See SRO/GD345/1005.

54. Some of the tiny panes of glass survive yet – a reminder of the relative cost of glass eg in 1797 a sheet of glass 12″ square cost 10d, whilst 2 sheets each 8½ square were only 6 1/2d—W. Nicol. *op. cit.* 1797. p.144.

55. Charles MacIntosh: *'Book of the Garden'* 1853 p.365.

56. William Lawson *"A New Orchard and Garden"* 1618 Reprint The Cresset Press Ltd. London, 1927 p.64.

57. Alexander Pope in a letter to the Guardian 29.9.1713.

58. Elsewhere boscage is used today on a small scale in contemporary gardens to form a maze—eg Cawdor Castle (site of a 16th Century holly maze and paradise gardens) and at Traquair. Both mazes were planted post 1975.

59. Graves of philosophers, terms, temples etc. could, at their highest, be read as symbols; this added an intellectual dimension, possibly even a moral one, to the tour of the wilderness and garden. NMRS FID/123/20 shows a painting of a 'moral landscape garden' at Craigtoun Park near St. Andrews where paths led out past follies to sites including the 'Island of Happiness' within the 'Lake of Tranquility' or else past 'Bad Education' or 'Self Love'.

60. Formal planting of specimen trees was retained in spectacular approach avenues eg the twin lines of sequoia at Benmore.

61. Japanese style lanterns can still be seen in gardens as distant as Manderston, Charleton and Kinloch Castle on Rhum.

62. John Macky: *op. cit.* Chapter 8 Perth. p.136.

63. The urn is inscribed in Latin, "Georgius Comes Arredonensis". MDCCCXLVII Havd Immemor".

64. Sir John Clerk of Penicuik *op. cit.* p.239.

65. D. McGibbon and T. Ross *'The Castellated and Domestic Architecture of Scotland'* vol. 5. p.442.

66. 'In this garden stands Queen Mary's Dial, which is a very curious one, but neglected' Defoe *op. cit.* 11/584. Thus the decline of interest in more complex dials may have begun as early as 1720. Aside from such facet-headed dials, 'lectern' dials with highly complex heads were tooled into a variety of shapes. One of the more elaborate examples remains in the walled garden at Culzean.

CHAPTER 3

67. Sir Archibald Grant of Monymusk *'Description of the Present state of (Monymusk) and what hath been done to make it what it is'* (1716). From the 'Miscellany of the Spalding Club' Volume 2 Aberdeen 1842 p.96.

68. Ochterlony of Guynd: *op. cit.* p.XIVI.

69. Ibid p.XIVI.

70. When Winton House, a one-time garrison of the Highlanders, was forfeited to the government in 1715 and passed to the infamous York Buildings Company, the 'fine gates and stone wall', symbols of the old regime, were demolished. Defoe *op. cit.* p.572.

71. See Soane museum Adam drawings Collection, Volume 34 page 68.

72. eg. at Kinross the generous box lodges built 1905 hark back to originals completed 1685 demolished 1810. There are modified box-lodges of interest at Saltoun Hall (joined by a crenellated bridge) and at Gosford (twin octagonal pavilions, elaborately detailed).

73. See NMRS PTD/122/1. This building has since been moved to allow for road widening.

74. Some of the other eccentric and unusual examples include the 'Jacobethan' screen at Meldrum House, the 'Egyptian-Gothick' construction at Dumfries House, the 'Garde-Bien' gateway at Tormaukin House and the great arch and screen wall at Rossdhu.

75. Christopher Hussey. *'The Work of Sir Robert Lorimer'* Country Life 1931. p.75.

76. The Brig o' Balgownie or Auld Brig o' Don spans a deep pool near the Cathedral in Aberdeen. Probably built in the early 14th century and restored in 1607, it is connected with a number of stories linked to witchcraft and also to William Bruce.

77. Dorothy Wordsworth: *op. cit.* p.131 Yet there was considerable efficiency. One barn in Glenshira could dry (on pins) 30 acres worth of the corn crop, another in Glen Era dried 45000 stone of hay 'this year'. James Robson *'A General View of Agriculture in the County of Argyll*, London. MDCCXCIV.

78. The Act was named after Montgomery, (1721–1803) Sponsor of the Act 10 Geo iii c 51.

79. John Martin Robinson *'Georgian Model Farms, A Study of Decorative and Model Farm Buildings in the Age of Improvement 1700–1846'* Clarendon Press, Oxford 1983. p.22.

80. Lucinda Lambton: *'The National Trust Book of Architecture for Animals. Beastly Buildings'*, Jonathan Cape 1985 p.124.

81. See NMRS KBD/64/7–20.

82. See NMRS CLD/27/9–10.

83. A number of dramatic doocots were built in association with courts of offices, for example at Stracathro. Fowl houses were also suggested e.g. by Daniel Mathie at Polmaise in 1786 (SRO RHP 3796/7) combining a pigeon house with accommodation for geese, turkeys, hens, ducks, calves and a little room for the henwife.

84. As well as kennel courtyards, many houses offered free-standing kennels blocks. A particularly good example in red and black masonry is at Spottiswoode, dated 1798, with subsequent Victorian additions.

CHAPTER 4

85. C Anne Williams: *'Food and Drink in Britain from the Stone Age to Recent Times.'* Constable. London. First Edition 1973. p.105.

86. Daniel Defoe: *op. cit.* Book 13. p.655.

87. Thomas Masters: *'The Ice Book'.* London 1844. Simpkin, Marshall and Co. p.50. Two of the many recipes therein read as follows: For coffee ice cream 'Take 6 of the best Turkey coffee berries, well roasted; put them on a tin, and place them in an oven for 5 minutes; boil 1 pint of cream and half a pint of milk together, and put them into a can; take the berries from the oven, and put them with the scalding cream; cover till cold. Strain, and add 1 ounce of arrow-root; boil, like custard, and add half a pound of sugar. Freeze. One quart. (p.96). For Nesselrode or Frozen Pudding 'Take one pint of cream, half a pint of milk, the yolks of 4 eggs, 1 ounce of sweet almonds pounded, and a half pound of sugar; put them in a stewpan on a gentle fire, set it thin as custard; when cold, add 2 wine glasses of nectar (a delicious beverage prepared only by the author). Freeze, and when sufficiently congealed, add 1 pound of preserved fruits, with a few currants; cut the fruit small, and mix well with the ice, and put it into little moulds, and immerse them in a freezing mixture, such as ice and salt etc until required for table. p.85.

88. An alternative arrangement visible at Kelburn, involved a flight of steps leading from ground level down into the chamber.

89. Ian G Lindsay and Mary Cosh: *'Inveraray and the Dukes of Argyll'*. Edinburgh University Press 1973. p.244.

90. See SRO RHP 1815.

91. For further information see Thomas Masters: *'A Short Treatise on the Production of Ice'* 1850.

92. Richard Pococke: *op. cit.* p.88.

93. For plans, see NMRS AGD/91/28, 53.

94. Ian G. Lindsay and Mary Cosh: *op. cit.* p.239.

95. For contemporary specification see SRO RHP 9714/58, 59.

96. Sir John Clerk of Penicuik: *op. cit.* p.239.

97. An 18th century sauce for salmon was prepared by boiling together vinegar, butter, ginger, parsley and sugar, whilst trout could be stuffed with a mixture of sorrell, parsley and 'and fine herbs' mixed with white wine and vinegar. See SRO GD 345/915/3.

98. Sir John Clerk of Penicuik: *op. cit.* p.239.

99. *'Journals of the Episcopal Visitations of the Right Rev. Robert Forbes 1762 and 1770'* edited by Rev. J. B. Craven, London MDCCCLXXXVI p.140.

100. Daniel Defoe: *op. cit.* p.571.

101. Gunpowder can be formed from a combination of sulphur, saltpetre and potassium nitrate. By boiling and cooling a solution of pigeon droppings in water, it was possible to crystallise out a suitable form of nitre.

102. See NMRS AGD/91/11,37.

103. By 1600 a number of doocots had been built combining a near square plan with a duopitched roof of stone slabs not unlike contemporary religious chapels—pure examples remain at New Spynie and Tealing.

104. Sir John Clerk of Penicuik *op. cit.* p.225. The present structure contains some 800 nesting boxes in a first floor cupola, reached by a spiral access stair from ground level. Within is a good example of a large potence in working order, with twin ladders giving access to all boxes. Camdens *'Britannia'* described the original thus: 'Built upon the the bank of the Carron a round house of polished stone, erected by Carausius' (Ninnius). In 1720 Dr. Stukely did a study which included drawings, prior to demolition of the building. Camden's *'Britannia'* vol. 2 London printed from 1722 edition, MDCCLXXII. p.282.

105. The finial on the roof of this doocot is in the form of a ship, rumoured to be the 'General Elliot' in which Captain Drummond of Megginch sailed to Macao, from where camelias were brought back.

CHAPTER 5

106. W. Wright: *'Grotesque Architecture'* 1767.

107. The Island Temple may have been associated with a triumphal arch now vanished. See Howard Colvin *'A Biographical Dictionary of British Architects 1600–1840'* John Murray 1978 p.58. The Bridge of Alvah was built adjacent to a Gothick tower.

108. 'This is called Diana's Grove, from a Statue of her with a Stag on rising ground, from which there are eight walks; below in the woods is a Temple of Fame, and on an Eminance in another part are the statues of three boys supporting a basket of flowers and fruit'. See Richard Pococke *op. cit.* p.230.

109. For example, see NMRS XSD/34/31 '3 Pavilions in Chinese style'.

110. Such artificial caves may have been designed for psychological catharsis but were really only extensions of natural caves on many estates, several of which were the subject of legend and folklore, appropriated at various times by the oppressed—the gypsies, the catholics, the Jacobites and the Covenanters. Celebrated examples include Archbishop Sharp's Cave at Scotscraig, Lady Charlotte's Cave at Dunkeld, and the caves below Culzean Castle.

111. Sir John Clerk. *op. cit.* p.239.

112. Ibid. p.221.

113. See SRO GD 18/5975.

114. *'Statistical Account of Scotland'* Volume 12 Lothian 1791–99. p.36.

115. Henry Skrine: *'Three Successive Tours in the North of England, to the Lakes and Great Part of Scotland'* 2nd Edition. London 1795. p.59.

116. Dorothy Wordsworth: *op. cit.* p.189.

117. Pennant: *op. cit.* p.119.

118. Dorothy Wordsworth: *op. cit.* p.210.

119. Ibid. *op. cit.* Part of the long 'Effusion in the Pleasure Ground on the Banks of the River Bran, near Dunkeld' Lines 13–17. p.294. Appendix E.

120. Skrine: *op. cit.* p.38.

121. Bishop Forbes. *op. cit.* p.239.

122. Dorothy Wordsworth *op. cit.* p.37.

123. Stories are all that remain of what may have been more elaborate structures such as the 'Willow Cathedral' built of reeds and willows in a rustic theme by Sir James Hall of Dunglass in 1794.

124. See SRO/RHP/961/2/1.

125. John Smith: *op. cit.* quoting Thomas Garnett p.83. Observations on a Tour through the Highlands 1800.

126. John Smith *op. cit.* p.58; see also NMRS PTD/127/143.

127. There were proposals possibly dated 1756/7 to add an elaborate gothick screen wall to the top of Duniquaich, see NMRS AGD/91/5, 65.

128. The original Eleanor Crosses, 12 in number, were erected by King Edward 1 in memory of his queen, Eleanor of Castiles, who died in 1290. The crosses marked the over-nighting stops of the funeral cortege as it passed from Harby near Lincoln to London. A number of copies were constructed in the nineteenth century.

129. Sir John Sinclair (who championed James MacPherson's claims about Ossian) took much credit for the production of the first *'Statistical Account of Scotland'* 1791–1799, in volume 18 of which he gives a lengthy description and line drawing of Harald's Tower.

130. Nine steps lead up to a first floor chamber below a slated ogee roof. Above the entry door, on a panel no longer legible, was carved:
    'Thou who desires ane humbling Sight to see come in behold What thou ere long must be.'

131. Robert Mitchell *'Plans and Views in Perspective with a Description of Buildings Erected in England and Scotland'* London 1801. p.5.

132. See SRO/GD112/20/5.

Selective Gazetteer

PLEASE NOTE THE MAJORITY OF THESE BUILDINGS ARE ON PRIVATE LAND AND ARE NOT OPEN TO THE PUBLIC. PERMISSION SHOULD ALWAYS BE OBTAINED BEFORE SEEKING ACCESS.

ABBOTSFORD NT5034 (73), Melrose, Borders
  Conservatory 1820, Formal gardens C19, Wall and Screen J. and T. Smith, Game Larder

ABERDOUR CASTLE NT1985 (65, 66), Aberdour, Fife
  Beehive doocot, Terraces 1572

ABERLOUR HOUSE NJ2743 (28), Aberlour, Grampian
  East Lodge 1838 William Roberston, West Lodge 1856 A. and W. Reid

ADEN NJ9847 (30), Old Deer, Grampian
  Round Square (half) late C18

ALLOA PARK NS8892 (58), Alloa, Central
  Great Garden 1706–14 6th Earl of Mar

ALVA NS8896 (58), Alva, Central
  Box Lodges proposed 1789 Robert Adam, Icehouse, Offices and Stables proposed Robert Adam, Stables 1805–9 William Stirling

AMISFIELD NT5275 (66), Haddington, Lothian
  Walled Garden 1783 John Henderson

ARBUTHNOTT NO7975 (45), Inverbervie, Grampian
  Garden Pavilian in C17 Formal Garden, Icehouse

ARDMADDY NM7816 (55), Kilninver, Strathcylde
  Boathouse 1795

ARNISTON NT3360 (66), Gorebridge, Lothian
  Box Lodges late C18, Cougar Gates 1766 installed 1824, Grotto 1726 William Adam, Orangery mid-C19, Wilderness 1726

AUCHINCRUIVE NS3823 (70), St Quivox, Strathcylde
  Tea Pavilion 1778 Robert Adam (Oswald's Temple)

BALBOUGHTY NO1227 (53, 58), New Scone, Tayside
  Dairy

BALCARRES NO4704 (59), Colinsburgh, Fife
  Gatelodge 1898 Sir Robert Lorimer

BALCASKIE NO5203 (59), St Monans, Fife
  Boscage c1850, Terraces C17 restored 1826, William Burn and W. S. Gilpin and 1844 W. A. Nesfield

BALFOUR HOUSE HY4716 (6), Shapinsay, Orkney
Doocot and Shower House C17 restored C19

BALLENCRIEF NS9770 (65), Aberlady, Lothian
Walled Garden 1524

BALLINDALLOCH CASTLE NJ1736 (28), Aberlour, Grampian
Gatelodge c1850 Thomas Mackenzie

BALMANNO NO1414 (58), Bridge of Earn, Tayside
Gatelodge Sir Robert Lorimer

BALMORAL NO2595 (37, 44), Crathie, Grampian
Dairy 1861 Prince Albert, Gamelarder 1860 Prince Albert, Various Cairns incl to
Prince Albert 1862

BARCLUITH NS7254 (64), Hamilton, Strathclyde
Terraces late C17

BEANSTON NT5476 (66), Haddington, Lothian
Orangery 1760

BLACKADDER MOUNT NT8553 (67, 74), Duns, Borders
Offices Alexander Boswell c1785

BLACK BARONY HOTEL NT2347 (73), Eddlestone, Borders
Temple C18, Relief Map of Scotland c1970

BLACKCRAIG NO1053 (53), Blairgowrie, Tayside
Gate/Bridge Patrick Allan Fraser over River Echt

BLAIR NN8765 (43), Blair Atholl, Tayside
Kitchen Garden c1750, Obelisk Tom-na-Croiche 1755, Temple of Fame 1745,
Wilderness 1737 part overlaid by 1850 pinetum, The Whim 1762 (pavilions may be
later)

BLAIR ADAM NT1295 (58), Kelty, Fife
Garden Pavilion

BOATH NH5773 (21), Auldearn, Highland
Doocot (restored NTS)

BORGUE NX6348 (83), Kirkcudbright, Dumfries and Galloway
Dairy 1901

BOWBUTTS NT3093 (59), Kirkcaldy, Fife
Doocot and Icehouse

BRECHIN CASTLE NO5959 (54), Brechin, Tayside
Walled Garden

BRIGLANDS NT0299 (58), Rumbling Bridge, Central
Gatelodge 1908 (dated 1898) Sir Robert Lorimer

BRODICK CASTLE NS0037 (69), Brodick, Arran
Rustic Summerhouse 1845

BROXMOUTH NT6977 (67), Dunbar, Lothian
Icehouse c1810

CADZOW CASTLE NS7353 (64), Hamilton, Strathclyde
Castle C15 altered to Picturesque Folly

CALLENDAR HOUSE NS8979 (65), Falkirk, Central
Mausoleum 1816 Archibald Elliot

CAMBUSWALLACE NN7103 (57), Doune, Central
Stables 1809 William Stirling

CAMPERDOWN PARK NO3632 (54), Dundee, Tayside
Walled Garden 1807 John Hay

CARNELL NS4632 (70), Hurlford, Strathclyde
Japanese Garden early C20

CASTLECRAIG NT1344 (72), Dolphinton, Borders
Box Lodges 1791

CASTLE KENNEDY NX1061 (82), Stranraer, Dumfries and Galloway
Two Boathouses c1850, Dancing Green, Mount Marlborough, Giants Grave c1720

CASTLE SEMPLE NS3760 (63), Lochwinnoch, Strathclyde
Peel Tower 1550, Prospect Tower 1770 Captain William McDowall

CHARLETON HOUSE NO4503 (59), Colinsburgh, Fife
Icehouse

CHATELHERAULT NS7353 (64), Hamilton, Strathclyde
Hunting Lodge 1732–42 William Adam

COCKENZIE HOUSE NT4075 (66), Cockenzie, Lothian
Gazebos, Hecla Sheil Pavilion c1783

COLZIUM HOUSE NS7278 (64), Kilsyth, Strathclyde
Icehouse c1680 re-used 1783, Gamepit

COWDEN NS9899 (58), Dollar, Central
Japanese Garden early C20 Ella Christie and Taki Honda

CRAIGEND NS5477 (64), Milngavie, Strathclyde
Smith's Folley

CRAIGIEHALL NT1675 (65, 66), Edinburgh, Lothian
Temple 1759 Charles Hope-Weir modified 1975

CRAIGMILLAR CASTLE NT2871 (66), Edinburgh, Lothian
Fishpond

CRAIGTOUN PARK SEE MOUNT MELVILLE

CRATHES CASTLE NO7396 (38, 45), Banchory, Grampian
Armillary Sundial, Boscage from 1702 and 1815, Doocot C17 relocated 1935 by Lady
Burnet, Planting Trough

CROSSRAGUEL ABBEY NS2708 (70), Maybole, Strathclyde
Beehive Doocot

CULLEN HOUSE NJ5066 (29), Cullen, Grampian
Entry Gates 1767 James Adam, Temple of Pomona 1788 completed 1822 William
Robertson

CULZEAN CASTLE NS2310 (70), Maybole, Strathclyde
Aviary post 1811, Bathhouse late C18, Camelia House James Donaldson 1818, Court of Offices 1780 Robert Adam restored 1973 Boys Jarvis, Chinese Pagoda 1860, Fortified Bridge c1780, Gardener's House, Goose House 1882, Icehouse c1780, Orangery c1850, Round House c1800, Walled Garden 1786 modified 1815, Rockery Grotto added 1870

DALDOWIE NS6162 (64), Glasgow, Strathclyde
Cylindrical Doocot

DALKEITH PALACE NT3367 (66), Dalkeith, Lothian
Conservatory 1832 William Burn, Montagu Bridge 1792 Robert Adam, Two Tunnels

DALLAS NJ1252 (23), Dallas, Grampian
Round Square late C17

DALMAHOY NT1467 (65), Ratho, Lothian
Lectern Doocot

DALMENY HOUSE NT1678 (65, 66), Queensferry, Lothian
Statue of King Tom 1873 Ernest Boehm

DALQUHARRAN CASTLE NS2702 (76), Maybole, Strathclyde
Offices and Stables proposed 1785 Robert Adam

DALZELL HOUSE NS7555 (64), Motherwell, Strathclyde
Japanese Gardens early C20

DARLEITH NS3480 (63), Alexandria, Strathclyde
Gardener's House

DIPPLE NJ3258 (28), Fochabers, Grampian
Dairy

DIRLETON CASTLE NT5184 (66), North Berwick, Lothian
Beehive Doocot C16 Ruthven period

DOUGARIE NR8837 (68, 69), Dougarie, Arran
Boathouse 1890 J. J. Burnet

THE DRUM NT3068 (66), Edinburgh, Lothian
Prospect Tower 1741 William Adam (demo)

DRUMLANRIG CASTLE NX8599 (78), Thornhill, Dumfries and Galloway
Parterres C17 restored C19 Charles M'Intosh, Rustic Summerhouses c1840 Charles M'Intosh

DRUMMOND CASTLE NN8418 (58), Crieff, Tayside
Italianate Garden 1789 developed 1820–40, Lewis Kennedy and J. C. Loudon, Sundial 1630 John Mylne

DRUMOAK NO7898 (38, 45), Aberdeen, Grampian
Walled Garden

DUDDINGSTONE HOUSE NT2972 (66), Edinburgh, Lothian
Offices 1763 Sir William Chambers, Rotunda 1768 Sir William Chambers

DUFF HOUSE NJ6963 (29), Banff, Grampian
Icehouse, Island Temple 1738 William Adam, Mausoleum c1790 James Duff, Walled Garden 1767 William Bowie

HOUSE OF DUN NO6659 (54), Montrose, Tayside
Gamelarder

DUNECHT HOUSE NJ7507 (38), Aberdeen, Grampian
East Gateway Marshall MacKenzie with gates 1923, Boathouse

DUNGLASS NT7671 (67), Cockburnspath, Lothian
Summerhouse 1718

DUNIPACE NS8083 (57, 65), Dunipace, Central
Doocot (former stairtower)

DUNKELD HOUSE NO0142 (52, 53), Dunkeld, Tayside
Chinese temple 1755 (demo), Hermitage, Ossian's Hall 1758 modified 1783 re-opened 1952 (NTS)

DUNMORE PARK NS8889 (65), Airth, Central
Mausoleum C15 converted 1802 datestones 1836-1943, The Pineapple 1761 Sir William Chambers

DUNROBIN CASTLE NC8500 (17), Golspie, Highland
Pavilion 1723, later modifications, Memorial to Harriet Duchess of Sutherland 1872

DUNS CASTLE NT7853 (67, 74), Duns, Borders
South Lodge 1820 James Gillespie Graham

DUNURE NS2515 (70), Maybole, Strathclyde
Beehive Doocot

EARLSHALL NO4621 (54, 59), Leuchars, Tayside
Topiary c1894, Walled Garden remodelled 1891 + Sir Robert Lorimer

EDZELL CASTLE NO5869 (44), Edzell, Tayside
Early C17 Walled Garden with Banqueting House and Bathhouse 1604 restored 1935 HBM, SDD

ERROL PARK NO2422 (53, 59), Errol, Tayside
Round Square 1811 with later additions

FAIRNALIE NT4533 (73), Selkirk, Borders
Pergolas J. J. Burnet

FASQUE NO6475 (45), Fettercairn, Grampian
Gothick Tower c1815 John Paterson

FINAVON CASTLE NO4957 (54), Forfar, Tayside
Lectern Doocot

FINGASK CASTLE NO2227 (53, 58), Rait, Tayside
Statues C19 by David and William Anderson, Sundial 1562, Topiary 1837-1882, Walled Garden c1790

FORMAKIN NS4070 (64), Bishopton, Strathclyde
Sundial Sir Robert Lorimer, Steading 1911 Sir Robert Lorimer

FOTHRINGHAM NO4644 (54), Forfar, Tayside
Doocot and Cattleshed

FULLARTON HOUSE NS3430 (70), Troon, Strathclyde
Offices and Stables proposed 1790 Robert Adam

FYVIE CASTLE NT7639 (29), Fyvie, Grampian
Boathouse 1816, Gatehouse 1819

GARTINCABER NN6900 (57), Thornhill, Central
Gothick Tower William Murdoch

GLAMIS CASTLE NO3846 (54), Glamis, Tayside
Gladiator, De'il and Church Lodge Gates 1680 relocated and modified 1774,
Italianate Garden 1907, Statues 1686 Arnold Quellin, Sundial 1671–80

THE GLEN NT2933 (73), Innerleithen, Borders
Fortified Gate

GORDON CASTLE NJ3559 (28), Fochabers, Grampian
Fountain 1540, Gatelodge early C19 Archibald Simpson, Orangery C19

GORDONSTOUN NJ1869 (28), Lossiemouth, Grampian
Round Square late C17 Sir Robert Gordon

GOSFORD HOUSE NT4578 (66), Aberlady, Lothian
Boathouse 1790, Grotto and Icehouse 1796 Alan Ramsey, Mausoleum 1794/5 Robert
Adam, Stables c1790 Robert Adam, West Gate 1854 R. W. Billings, North Lodges
1857 R. W. Billings

GUISACHAN HOUSE NH2825 (25), Cannich, Highland
Dairy

GUTHRIE CASTLE NO5650 (54), Forfar, Tayside
Boscage, Walled Garden

HADDO HOUSE NT8634 (30), Methlick, Grampian
Obelisk post 1815, Urn 1867

HAMILTON PALACE NS7256 (64), Hamilton, Strathclyde
Mausoleum 1843 David Bryce, Rotunda 1869 Charles Wilson

HARVIESTOUN CASTLE NS9397 (58), Dollar, Central
East and West Lodges

HATTON HOUSE NT1268 (65), Ratho, Lothian
Bathhouse, Gateway 1692 repositioned 1829, Gazebos

HILL OF TARVIT NO3811 (59), Cupar, Fife
Boscage, Farmstead

HODDOM CASTLE NY1573 (85), Ecclefechan, Dumfries and Galloway
Repentance Tower 1560

HOLYROOD HOUSE NT2673 (66), Edinburgh, Lothian
Fountain 1859 Charles Doyle, Queen Mary's Bathhouse C16, Sundial 1633 John
Mylne

HOPETOUN HOUSE NT0879 (65), South Queensferry, Lothian
Staneyhill Tower C17, Sphinxes

185

HOSPITALFIELD NO6240 (54), Arbroath, Tayside
Fernery c1870 Patrick Allan Fraser, Home Farm Patrick Allan Fraser

HOUSE OF THE BINNS NT0578 (65), Linlithgow, Lothian
Waterloo Tower 1826 Alexander Allen

HUNTINGTON HOUSE NT4874 (66), Haddington, Lothian
Pavilion Doocot c1750

INVERARAY NN0908 (56), Inveraray, Strathclyde
Beehive Cottage 1802-3 Alexander Nasmyth, Bealachanuanan Grotto 1747 William
Adam, Bridge Roger Morris/William Adam, Bridge Robert Mylne, Boathouse on
Loch Dhu 1752 (demo), Carloonan Doocot 1748 Roger Morris, Duniquaich Wat-
chtower 1745 John Adam and Roger Morris, Icehouse 1786 William Stothard, Maam
Steading 1796 Robert Mylne, The Hexagon 1802-3 Alexander Nasmyth, Stables at
Cherry Park 1758 John Adam, Tombreac Dairy 1753 John Adam modified later,
Pump House 1760, Walled Garden James Potter

INVERMAY NO0616 (58), Dunning, Tayside
Doocot and Tea House 1801-5 (moved 1960), Walled Garden Walter Nicol c1802

INVERQUHOMERY NK0246 (30), Longside, Grampian
Three Gothick Doocots early C19

JOHNSTOUNBURN NT4661 (66), Humbie, Lothian
Apple House C18, Lectern Doocot C18

KEIR HOUSE NS7698 (57), Bridge of Allan, Central
Bathing House 1893, South Lodge 1820 David Hamilton (moved), Steading 1832
David Bryce and others (including 1856-61 Sir William Stirling Maxwell), Swan Gate
mid C19

KELBURN CASTLE NS2156 (63), Largs, Strathclyde
Sundial early C18

KELLIE CASTLE NO5205 (59), Arncroach, Fife
Pigeon 'Fuie' Sir Robert Lorimer, Treillage Fencing Sir Robert Lorimer

KILDRUMMY CASTLE NJ4516 (37), Rhynie, Grampian
Copy of Brig o' Balgownie in 1904 Japanese Gardens

KINFAUNS CASTLE NO1522 (53, 58), Perth, Tayside
Dairy 1928 Sir Robert Lorimer, Kinnoul and Binhill Towers post 1813, 9th Earl of
Kinnoul

KINKELL CASTLE NH5554 (26), Cononbridge, Highland
Moon Viewing Pavilion c1970

KINLOCH CASTLE NM4099 (39), Rhum
Burial Vault late C19 (demo), Mausoleum

KINNAIRD CASTLE NO6357 (54), Brechin, Tayside
Rustic Summerhouse 1800 Lady Carnegie

KINROSS HOUSE NO1202 (58), Kinross, Tayside
Fish Gate C17 Peter Paul Boyce and Cornelius van Nerven, Court of Offices 1690
Sir William Bruce

KIRKDALE HOUSE NX5153 (83), Creetown, Dumfries and Galloway
Offices and Stables proposed 1785 Robert Adam

LANRICK NN6903 (57), Doune, Tayside
Golden Gate c1870 James Campbell Walker, MacGregor Memorial early C19 Sir Euan Murray MacGregor, Offices and Stables c1790

LARGO HOUSE NO4203 (59), Upper Largo, Fife
Court of Offices c1750, Gatepiers c1750

LEITCHESTON NJ4062 (28), Fochabers, Grampian
Lectern Doocot

LEITH HALL NJ5429 (37), Rhynie, Grampian
Moon Gate

LENNOXLOVE NT5172 (66), Haddington, Lothian
Sundial 1679

LINLITHGOW PALACE NS9977 (65), Linlithgow, Lothian
King's Fountain c1530 James V reconstructed c1930

LITTLE SPARTA NT0748 (72), Dunsyre, Strathclyde
Sundials Ian Hamilton Finlay c1985

LOCHINCH SEE CASTLE KENNEDY

LOCHNELL HOUSE NM8838 (49), Barcaldine, Strathclyde
Lady Margaret's Tower 1754 Lady Campbell of Lochnell

LOGAN HOUSE NX0941 (82), Port Logan, Dumfries and Galloway
Fishpond modifies 1800 Andrew McDowall

LUFFNESS NT4780 (66), Aberlady, Lothian
Doocot and Water Tower, Icehouse 1847, Walled Garden c1800

LUNDIN TOWER NO4002 (59), Lundin Links, Fife
Doocot modified 1800

MACBIEHILL NT1851 (65, 66), West Linton, Lothian
Mausoleum of Massy Beresfords 1769 repaired 1974

MANDERSTON NT8154 (67, 74), Duns, Borders
Boathouse 1894, Gardener's House 1897, Marble Dairy c1900 John Kinross, Stables 1905 John Kinross

MAVISBANK NT2865 (66), Loanhead, Lothian
Walled Garden 1739

MEET HILL HOUSE NK1145 (30), Peterhead, Grampian
Reform Tower 1832

MEGGINCH CASTLE NO2424 (53, 59), Errol, Tayside
Arcaded Doocot and Gothick Court 1809, Topiary Crown 1887 Lady Drummond, Twin Lodges 1809 and earlier obelisk garepiers, Walled Garden 1575 modified 1780

MELDRUM HOUSE NJ8129 (38), Oldmeldrum, Grampian
Gazebos

MELLERSTAIN NT6439 (74), Kelso, Borders
Doocot converted to Cottage Ornée 1825 (Robert Smirke) restored 1978, Hundy Mundy c1775, Italianate Garden 1909 Sir Reginald Blomfield, Mausoleum 1736 George Baillie Hamilton

MELVILLE HOUSE NO2913 (59), Collessie, Fife
Doocot former mill, Gazebos 1697

MILLEARN NN9317 (58), Auchterarder, Tayside
Dairy Richard Dickson

MILTON-LOCKHART NS8149 (72), Carluke, Strathclyde
Fortified Bridge

MONTEVIOT HOUSE NT6424 (74), Ancrum, Borders
Baron's Folley, Mausoleum 1864 Sir Thomas Monteith, Penielhaugh 1815 Archibald Elliot

MONZIE CASTLE NN8724 (52, 58), Crieff, Tayside
Gate/Bridge John Paterson

MORTONHALL NT2668 (66), Edinburgh, Lothian
Icehouse

MOUNIE CASTLE NJ7628 (38), Oldmeldrum, Grampian
Doocot converted to Garden House Sir Robert Lorimer

MOUNTHOOLY NJ9266 (30), Rosehearty, Grampian
Doocot

MOUNT MELVILLE NO4714 (59), St Andrews, Fife
Boathouse Paul Waterhouse (demo), Pergolas Paul Waterhouse (demo)

MURDOSTOUN CASTLE NS8257 (65, 72), Wishaw, Strathclyde
Doocot and Icehouse 1790

MURTHLY CASTLE NO0739 (52, 53), Dunkeld, Tayside
Banqueting House 1669, Malakoff Arch (demo)

NETHERBYRES NT9463 (67), Eyemouth, Borders
Walled Garden 1740

NETHERURD NT1044 (72), Dolphinton, Lothian
Whalebone Gate 1795 William Burn, rebuilt 1959

NEWARK CASTLE NS3374 (63), Port Glasgow, Strathclyde
Beehive Doocot

NEWBATTLE ABBEY NT3366 (66), Eskbank, Lothian
Two Sundials 1635

NEWHAILES NT3272 (66), Musselburgh, Lothian
Grotto 1792

NEWTON DON NT7037 (74), Kelso, Borders
Rustic Garden Seat

NISBET HILL NT7950 (67, 74), Duns, Borders
Pavilion Doocot

NOVAR HOUSE NH6167 (21), Invergordon, Highland
Gate of Negrapatam c1790

OATFIELD HOUSE NR6818 (68), Campbeltown, Strathclyde
Grotto

PANMURE HOUSE NO5137 (54), Carnoustie, Tayside
The Testimonial 1839 John Henderson, Tower 1694

PARK HOUSE NO7797 (38, 45), Stonehaven, Grampian
Walled Garden c1835 Archibald Simpson

PENICUIK HOUSE NT2159 (66, 73), Penicuik, Lothian
Arthur's O'on 1760 Sir John Clerk, Bathhouse 'Clare Hall' Sir John Clerk,
Hurleycove Tunnel 1742 Sir John Clerk, Icehouse, Stables 1760 modified early C20,
Terregles Tower 1748–52 Sir John Clerk, Obelisk to Allan Ramsay 1759 Sir John
Clerk, Walled Garden pre 1730, Walled Garden 1870

PHANTASSIE NT5977 (67), East Linton, Lothian
Doocot C16 restored NTS

PITKERRO NO4533 (54), Dundee, Tayside
Gatelodge 1903 Sir Robert Lorimer

PITFOUR NK9743 (30), Old Deer, Grampian
Bathhouse 'Temple of Theseus' 1830, Boathouse c1830, Bridge c1820, Observation
Tower 1845 Admiral Ferguson

PITMEDDEN NJ8828 (38), Ellon, Grampian
Gazebos C17, Great Garden 1675 Alexander Seton restored NTS, Sundial 1675

HOUSE OF PITMUIES NO5649 (54), Forfar, Tayside
Doocot

POLLOK HOUSE NS5461 (64), Glasgow, Strathclyde
Terraces and Gazebos C19 Rowand Anderson

PRESTONFIELD HOUSE NT2771 (66), Edinburgh, Lothian
Round Square 1816 James Gillespie Graham

PRESTON HALL NT3965 (66), Pathhead, Lothian
Box Lodges 1795 Robert Mitchell, Garden Pavilions 1795 Robert Mitchell,
Mausoleum 1795 Robert Mitchell

RAEHILLS NY0694 (78), Lockerbie, Dumfries and Galloway
Three-Arm Bridge

RAITH PARK NT2592 (59), Kirkcaldy, Fife
Gamelarder, Lookout Tower

RAVELSTON HOUSE NT2274 (66), Edinburgh, Lothian
Lectern Doocot, Fountain 1630

ROSEBERY NT3057 (66, 73), Temple, Lothian
Steading c1800 Archibald John Primrose, 4th Earl of Rosebery

ROSEHAUGH NH6855 (26), Fortrose, Highland
Dairy 1907 William Flockart

ROSSDHU HOUSE NS3689 (56), Luss, Strathclyde
  Icehouse

SALTOUN HALL NT4668 (66), East Saltoun, Lothian
  Pavilion Doocot late C19, Offices

SCHAW PARK NS9094 (58), Alloa, Central
  Doocot former mill

SCONE PALACE NO1126 (53, 58), Perth, Tayside
  Mausoleum 1784 modified 1807 William Atkinson, Pinetum 1848

SPOTTISWOODE NT6049 (74), Lauder, Borders
  Two 'Magical Arches'

STIRLING CASTLE NS7993 (57), Stirling, Central
  King's Knot 1625 William Watts

STOBO CASTLE NT1736 (72), Peebles, Borders
  Icehouse, Japanese Garden early C20 Hylton Philipson

STRACATHRO HOUSE NO6265 (45), Brechin, Tayside
  Bridge 1828 William Atkinson

STRATHLEVEN HOUSE NS3977 (63), Alexandria, Strathclyde
  Pavilion Doocot C18

STROMA ND3577 (7), Camisbay, Stroma
  Doocot and Burial Vault

TANTALLON CASTLE NT5985 (67), North Berwick, Lothian
  Lectern Doocot C16-C17

TAYMOUTH CASTLE NN7846 (51, 52), Kenmore, Tayside
  Fort 1760-1774 John Baxter (John Paterson), Gatelodges including Fort Lodge,
  Delarb Lodge, Rock Lodge, Kenmore Arch, Dairy c1840 James Gillespie Graham,
  Hermitage at Falls of Acharn, Queen Eleanor Cross 1831 William Atkinson, Venus
  Temple demolished 1830, Walled Garden with gate dated 1838 J. Smith

TEALING NO4138 (54), Dundee, Tayside
  Doocot 1595 MBM (SDD)

THIRLESTANE CASTLE NT5347 (73), Lauder, Borders
  Terraces David Bryce

THURSO CASTLE ND1268 (12), Thurso, Highland
  Gateway c1875 Donald Leed, Haralds Tower 1970 Sir John Sinclair, Mausoleum of
  Sinclairs of Ulbster

TILLICOULTRY HOUSE NS9297 (58), Tillicoultry, Central
  Stable early C19

TOROSAY NM7235 (49), Craignure, Mull
  Terraces and Gazebos, Statue Walk 1900 (includes work by Antonio Bonazza
  1698 +)

TRAQUAIR HOUSE NT3235 (73), Innerleithen, Borders
  Fountain C19 Sun Foundry, Gates 1737, Bears added 1745, Gazebos c1664 James
  Smith, Rustic Summerhouse 1834

TYNINGHAME NT6179 (67), Dunbar, Lothian
    Boscage, Obelisk 1856 6th Earl of Haddington, St Baldred's Chapel C12 demo
    c1750, Treillage Pavilion c1970

URY HOUSE NO8587 (45), Stonehaven, Grampian
    Ink Bottle Lodges c1860

WEYMYSS CASTLE NT3395 (59), Coaltown of Wemyss, Fife
    Gatepiers

WHIM HOUSE NT2153 (73), West Linton, Borders
    Icehouse c1745, Stables late C18

YESTER HOUSE NT5467 (66), Gifford, Lothian
    Gardener's House, Grotto 1708, St Cuthbert's Chapel C15 modified 1753 Robert
    Adam, Summerhouse of glazed clocktower from old Caledonian Railway Station,
    Edinburgh, erected 1970

PLAN OF THE HOUSE AND GARDENS AT NEWLISTON, 1759 (p 11)
NOTATION: A House, B Forecourt, C Terrace Walk, D Entry to House, E Back Court,
F Kitchen Gardens, G Bowling Green, H 'Necessary House', J Bank round Bowling
Green, K Broad Walk, L View to Lindsays Craigs, M View to Craigie Hall, N Vista,
P Pigeon House, Q Wilderness, R Two Amphitheatres, S Canals and Pond, T Little Park,
U Serpentine Walk
The garden is surrounded by stone walls; dotted areas denote tree planting, lined areas
show water.

PLAN OF THE OFFICES PROPOSED FOR ALVA HOUSE, c1790 (p 97)
NOTATION: A Bakehouse, B Boiling Room, C Brewhouse, D Cartshed, E Coach
House, F Cowhouse, G Dairy, H Drying Yard, J Dung Pit, K Entrance, L Henhouse,
M Pighouse, N Poultryhouse, P Scullery, Q Slaughterhouse, R Smith and Carpenter,
S Stables, T Steward, V Washhouse and Laundry, W Water, X Yard

Acknowledgements

This book is the culmination of a study begun in 1982 when the author was completing the Patrick Plunket Memorial Scholarship from the Society for the Protection of Ancient Buildings. It was given further impetus in 1983 with the award of the Thomas Ross Prize from the Royal Incorporation of Architects in Scotland.

The author gratefully acknowledges with thanks the considerable assistance and encouragement of Charles McKean and the Royal Incorporation of Architects in Scotland without whom this book would not have been published. The author is similarly grateful for the invaluable help of Kitty Cruft and Ian Gow of the National Monuments Record (Scotland) and David Walker of Historic Buildings and Monuments.

The contribution is also acknowledged of the many representatives of Local Authority Planning and Conservation departments at Regional and District level who were kind enough to provide information. Many courteous land owners, factors, gardeners and farmers were good enough to help in the field and in some cases allow access into archives.

Academic research has been greatly assisted by facilities and staff in the following organisations and institutions:

In Edinburgh: The Central Library, Historic Buildings and Monuments, the Library and Drawings Collection of the Royal Incorporation of Architects in Scotland, The National Library of Scotland, the National Monuments Record (Scotland), The National Trust for Scotland, The Royal Commission on the Ancient and Historical Monuments of Scotland, the Search Rooms of the Scottish Record Office at Register House and at West Register House.

In London: The British Library, Sir John Soane's Museum, the Library and Drawings Collection of the Royal Institute of British Architects.

The great majority of photographs and drawings are by the author. However, credits and thanks are also due to the following. Mr Keith Adam, Sir John Clerk of Penicuik, Charles McKean, Stewart Tod, the Trustees of the Tenth Duke of Argyll, The Trustees of the National Library of Scotland, The National Trust for Scotland, The Royal Commission on the Ancient and Historic Monuments of Scotland.

In the course of research a number of people lent support at various times including staff at the Edinburgh University School of Architecture, Ruth Burgess, Keith Dowse, David Pearce, David Schofield, James Simpson, Allison Walker, Fred and Mardy Walker. Also my mother. My father maintained a keen interest in this study until his death in 1988.

In spite of all this help, errors and inaccuracies in the text must remain the responsibility of the author.